PROPHETS AND KINGS

DISCOVERY GUIDE

**That the World May Know®
with Ray Vander Laan**

PROPHETS AND KINGS

—————— 6 LESSONS ON ——————

Being in the Culture
and Not of It

DISCOVERY GUIDE

**EXPERIENCE THE BIBLE IN
HISTORICAL CONTEXT™**
Ray Vander Laan
with Stephen and Amanda Sorenson

 ZONDERVAN®

 FOCUS ON THE FAMILY

ZONDERVAN

Prophets and Kings Discovery Guide
Copyright © 1999, 2008 by Ray Vander Laan

This title is also available as a Zondervan ebook. Visit www.zondervan.com/ebooks.

Requests for information should be addressed to:
Zondervan, 3900 Sparks Dr. SE, Grand Rapids, Michigan 49546

Focus on the Family and the accompanying logo and design are federally registered trademarks
of Focus on the Family, 8605 *Explorer Drive, Colorado Springs, Colorado 80920.*

That the World May Know is a trademark of Focus on the Family.

ISBN 978-0-310-87878-0

All maps are courtesy of International Mapping.

All artwork is courtesy of Ray Vander Laan unless otherwise indicated.

All Scripture quotations are taken from The Holy Bible, *New International Version®, NIV.*®
Copyright © 1973, 1978, 1984 by Biblica, Inc.® Used by permission. All rights reserved worldwide.

Any Internet addresses (websites, blogs, etc.) and telephone numbers in this book are offered
as a resource. They are not intended in any way to be or imply an endorsement by Zondervan,
nor does Zondervan vouch for the content of these sites and numbers for the life of this book.

Cover design: Do**More**Good®
Cover photography: BiblePlaces.com
Interior design: Ben Fetterley, Denise Froehlich

Printed in the United States of America

CONTENTS

CONTENTS

INTRODUCTION

Because God speaks to us through the Scriptures, studying them is a rewarding experience. The inspired human authors of the Bible, as well as those to whom the words were originally given, were primarily Jews living in the ancient Near East. God's words and actions spoke to them with such power, clarity, and purpose that they wrote them down and carefully preserved them as an authoritative body of literature.

God's use of human servants in revealing himself resulted in writings that clearly bear the stamp of time and place. The message of the Scriptures is, of course, eternal and unchanging — but the circumstances and conditions of the people of the Bible are unique to their times. Consequently, we most clearly understand God's truth when we know the cultural context within which he spoke and acted and the perception of the people with whom he communicated.

This does not mean that God's revelation is unclear if we don't know the cultural context. Rather, by learning how to think and approach life as the people of the Bible did, modern Christians will deepen their appreciation and understanding of God's Word. Unfortunately, many Christians today do not have even a basic knowledge of the world and people of the Bible. This series is designed to help solve that problem. We will be studying the people and events of the Bible in their geographical, historical, and cultural contexts.

Although the DVD segments offer the latest archaeological research, this series is not intended to be a definitive historical, cultural, or geographical study of the lands and times of the Bible. No original scientific discoveries are revealed here. My goal is simply to help us better understand the message of the Bible. Once we know the *who*, *what*, and *where* of a Bible story, we will be able to better understand the *why*. By deepening our understanding of God's Word, we can more clearly see God's revealed mission for our lives and strengthen our relationship with him.

The Assumptions of Biblical Writers

For this study, it is important to realize that people today use the names *Israel* and *Palestine* to designate the land God gave to Abraham and that both terms are politically charged. *Palestine* is used by the Arabs living in the central part of the country, while *Israel* is used by the Jews to indicate the State of Israel. In this study, however, *Israel* is used in the biblical sense. This choice does not indicate a political statement regarding the current struggle in the Middle East, but is chosen because it best reflects the biblical designation for the land.

Biblical writers assumed that their readers were familiar with Near Eastern geography, history, and culture. They used a language which, like all languages, is bound by culture and time. For example, the people whom God chose as his instruments — the people to whom he revealed himself — lived in the Near East, where people typically described their world and themselves in concrete terms. Their language was one of pictures, metaphors, and examples rather than ideas, definitions, and abstractions.

This is why the Bible is filled with concrete images. While we might describe God as omniscient or omnipresent (knowing everything and present everywhere), the people of the Bible would have preferred to describe God by saying, "The Lord is my Shepherd," or "God is our Father, and we are his children," or "God is the Potter, and we are the clay." So to understand the Scriptures, we need to know more than what the words mean, we need to understand them from the perspective of the people who thought and spoke in terms of those images every day of their lives. We need to know what it meant for them to recognize Jesus as the Lamb killed on Passover, and to think of heaven in terms of an oasis in the desert and hell being like a city sewage dump.

The people of the Bible also had an Eastern mind-set rather than a Western mind-set. Eastern thought emphasizes the process of learning as much as or more than the result. Whereas Westerners tend to collect information to find the right answer, Hebrew thought stresses the process of discovery as well as the answer. So as you go through this study, use it as an opportunity to deepen your understanding of who God is and to grow in your relationship with him.

Understanding the World of the Hebrews

More than 3,800 years ago, God spoke to his servant Abraham: "Go, walk through the length and breadth of the land, for I am giving it to you" (Genesis 13:17). From the outset, God's choice of a Hebrew nomad to begin his plan of salvation (a plan that is still unfolding today) was linked to the selection of a specific land where his redemptive work would take place. The nature of God's covenant relationship with his people demanded a place where their faith could be exercised and displayed to all nations so that the world would know of *Yahweh*, the true and faithful God.

The Promised Land, then, was the arena in which God's people were to serve him faithfully as the world watched. So if we are to fully understand God's plan and purpose for his people, we must also understand the nature of the place he selected for them. After all, God showed the same care in preparing a land for his chosen people as he did in preparing a people to live in that land.

The land God chose for his people was on the crossroads of the world. A major trade route of the ancient world, the Via Maris, ran through the land, and more than a million people a year traveled that route. God intended for the Israelites to take control of the cities along this route and thereby exert influence on the nations around them. Through their righteous living, the Hebrews were to reveal the one true God, *Yahweh*, to the world. (They failed to accomplish this mission, however, because of their unfaithfulness.)

Western Christianity tends to spiritualize the concept of the Promised Land as it is presented in the Bible. Instead of seeing it as a crossroads from which to influence the world, modern Christians tend to view it as a distant, heavenly city, a glorious "Canaan" toward which we are traveling as we ignore the world around us. We focus more on the destination than the journey and, in a sense, view our earthly experience as simply preparation for an eternity in the "promised land." We have unconsciously separated our walk with God from our responsibility to the world in which he has placed us, which distorts our perception of the mission God has set for us.

Many Christians today have forgotten that the mission of God's people has always been to live *so that the world would know that*

their God was the true God. This was true when the Hebrews left
Egypt and possessed the Promised Land. It was true during the years
of the exile in Babylon. It was true during the time Jesus lived on
earth after the Jews had returned to Israel. And it was true for the
disciples of Jesus who followed him as their Rabbi and obeyed his
command to go out into the world and make disciples.

The life of faith is not a vague, otherworldly experience. Rather, it is
being faithful to God right now, in the place and time in which he
has put us. This truth is emphasized by God's choice of Canaan, a
crossroads of the ancient world, as the Promised Land in which the
Israelites were to live. Our mission as Christians today is the same
one God gave to the Israelites when they possessed the Promised
Land, the same one Jesus gave to his disciples. We are to love the
Lord our God with all our heart, with all our soul, and with all our
might, and to love our neighbors as ourselves so that through us *the
world may know that our God is the one true God.*

INNOCENT BLOOD – PART ONE

Tel Megiddo, where this session was filmed, is located at a strategic mountain pass overlooking the Plain of Jezreel, which made the city of Megiddo one of the most important cities in ancient Israel. The Via Maris, the main trade route between the dominant world powers of the day — Egypt and the Mesopotamian empires of Assyria, Babylon, and Persia — crossed the mountains at Megiddo. So whoever controlled the city could exert great power over world trade and have significant influence over world culture.

In fact, the Via Maris was one source of Solomon's wealth because God gave him the political might to control the key cities along that trade route — Hazor, Gezer, and of course Megiddo. Some scholars believe that because of Megiddo's strategic location more battles have been fought in the Jezreel Valley below it than in any other place in the world. But in the context of the Bible, Megiddo represents more than political control, more than economic and cultural influence. It also represents the battle for spiritual control of the minds and hearts of people — the ongoing battle between good and evil. That battle was waged when the people of ancient Israel lived in the land, it continues to this day, and it will culminate in the battle of *Har Megiddo*, or Armageddon. So let's take a closer look at the significance of Tel Megiddo.

Centuries before the Israelites settled in the Promised Land (from about 2950 - 2350 BC), Megiddo was a prominent "high place" where the people of Canaan worshiped their fertility god, Baal, and his supposed mistress, Asherah. The Canaanite worship practices demonstrated a blatant disregard for human life and God's laws concerning human sexuality, so when the Israelites settled in the land, their beliefs and values clashed with those of the Canaanite residents.

Over time, however, the lure of Canaanite culture induced the Israelites to participate in the worship of Baal and Asherah. These fertility gods, whom the Canaanites credited with providing rain for the lush crops of the Jezreel Valley, had an appeal that the God of Israel, whom the people of Israel knew primarily as the God of the desert wilderness, did not have. As time passed, the worship practices of the Canaanites became more and more a part of life for the Israelites. Even Israel's kings — especially King Ahab and his wife, Jezebel (who had been a priestess of Baal in her homeland of Phoenicia) — encouraged Baal worship.

The rituals of Baal worship included sexual intercourse with temple prostitutes and the sacrifice of infants in order to induce the gods to send rain for the crops. Thus, the Israelites engaged in detestable acts and even sacrificed their children in order to ensure personal gain and success. These practices perverted two of the most beautiful gifts God gave humankind: human life and the sexual relationship between a husband and wife within the bonds of marriage. The horror of these abominable practices that stand in opposition to God's commands will challenge us to consider ways in which we also pervert God's gifts.

NOTE: Because of the length and nature of the material covered in this video presentation we'll take two sessions to complete the study. Part one will involve viewing the entire segment followed by Bible Discovery and Discussion. Part two will begin with a DVD reviewfollowed by Bible Discovery and Discussion.

Opening Thoughts (3 minutes)

The Very Words of God

> Be very strong; be careful to obey all that is written in the Book of the Law of
> Moses, without turning aside to the right or to the left. Do not associate with
> these nations that remain among you; do not invoke the names of their gods
> or swear by them. You must not serve them or bow down to them. But you
> are to hold fast to the LORD your God.

Joshua 23:6 – 8

Think About It

God's people have always been participants in the great spiritual
battle between good and evil — between the values of God and
the values of Satan. The battle for control of our hearts, minds, and
souls continues to take place today just as it did for God's people in
ancient times.

In which area(s) of your life are you most aware of the battle
between good and evil? In what ways do you think the battle you
face is like or unlike the battle faced by the people you read about in
the Bible?

DVD Teaching Notes (33 minutes)

Megiddo:

A place of significance

Battleground for control of the world

Baal worship:
  The practices

The significance for Israel

The significance for us

DVD Discussion (5 minutes)

1. Which images and/or thoughts made the most powerful impressions on you? Why?

2. What similarities do you see between the culture in which you live and the Canaanite culture?

How would you compare the ways in which you respond to and interact with your culture to the ways in which the ancient Israelites responded to and interacted with Canaanite culture?

Small Group Bible Discovery and Discussion (10 minutes)

The Battle for Control — More Than Just Survival

Life in the ancient Near East was not easy. In order to survive, multiply, and prosper, people needed physical safety, water, food, and resources such as fertile land, fertile flocks, and families. Before they ever set foot in the Promised Land, God assured his people that he would provide these essentials — and give them abundantly — if they would be faithful to worship and obey him always (Deuteronomy 11). But the people who occupied Canaan believed that such gifts of life came from another source: Baal and his mistress, Asherah. The ensuing clash of beliefs and values between the Canaanites and the Israelites was not only a battle for survival in their environment; it was a battle with far-reaching spiritual implications: a battle for the hearts, minds, and souls of God's people.

1. What did King Solomon do at Hazor, Megiddo, and Gezer? (See 1 Kings 9:15 - 17.)

Why was it important for Solomon to build walls around the three main cities along the Via Maris in Israel?

Discuss the possible political, financial, cultural, and spiritual impact of these improvements.

DATA FILE
The Via Maris — Lifeline of Civilizations
Why It Was Vital

In ancient times, Egypt (to the southwest of Israel) and the Mesopotamian empires of Assyria, Babylon, and Persia (to the northeast of Israel) required the exchange of vital goods. Whoever controlled the road between these empires dominated international trade and exerted great influence on other cultures. The rugged mountain ranges of Samaria, Judea, and Hebron cut through the middle of Israel, making east-west travel difficult. The hostile Arabian Desert to the east of the Jordan River added to the transportation difficulties. So the easiest route for commerce between the great civilizations of the ancient Near East took a north-south track through Israel.

Its Location

The Via Maris entered the Great Rift Valley in Israel from the east, near Mount Hermon, and continued to the Sea of Galilee. Then it turned southwest across the Valley of Jezreel and cut through the ridge of Mount Carmel to reach the coastal plain. Only one of three passes through the Mount Carmel ridge provided relatively easy travel: the Iron Wadi, which was guarded by Megiddo. Once past Mount Carmel, the road continued toward Egypt. The main route followed the coast several miles inland, which enabled travelers to avoid the swamplands where runoff from the Judah Mountains was trapped by coastal sand dunes.

Its Control Points

The Via Maris could be controlled easily from three key points in Israel: Gezer, Hazor, and Megiddo. Gezer stood where the road passed between swamplands and mountains. Hazor and Megiddo stood where the road entered mountain passes. Megiddo guarded the most narrow pass, which made it the most strategic point. However, the Israelites generally feared the Philistines and Canaanites who occupied the territory around Gezer and Megiddo, so they settled in the nearby foothills and rarely controlled these key cities. As a result, they never exerted the degree of influence on world culture that God intended them to have.

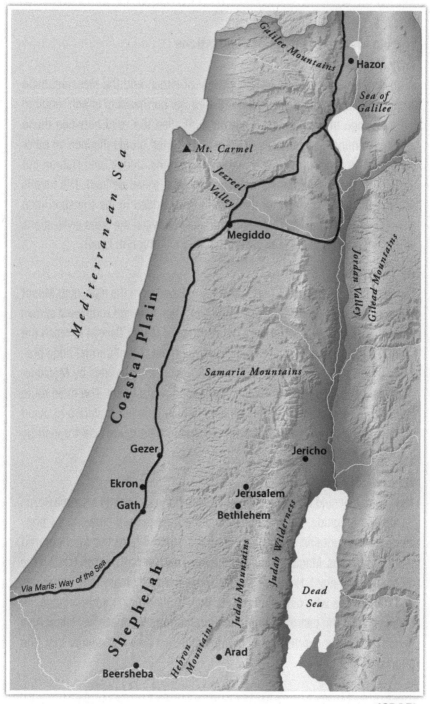

ISRAEL

2. What measures did the people of Megiddo take to ensure their water supply? (See Data File: Water Systems of Old Testament Times below)

    What benefits did a secure water supply provide for the people?

    Discuss the ways in which a secure water supply might have influenced the beliefs and values of the people.

DATA FILE
Water Systems of Old Testament Times
In the arid region of Israel, water has always been important to its inhabitants. During ancient times, people spent a good part of their day obtaining water, and cities were built only where fresh water existed. When a city was small, a nearby spring, well, or cistern was sufficient. But as a city grew in size and political significance, its inhabitants took steps to protect their water supply.

continued on next page . . .

During Solomon's time, for example, a wall or corridor often extended from the city wall to the nearby spring or well. But this setup was vulnerable to extended sieges. Sometime during the late ninth or early eighth century BC, a new technology emerged: the water shaft. People would dig a shaft to reach the water table and—sometimes using a horizontal tunnel—would direct the water into the city.

ENTRANCE TO THE WATER SHAFT ON TEL MEGIDDO

Scholars believe that during the ninth century BC, the inhabitants of Megiddo dug a square, vertical shaft more than 115 feet deep that connected to a horizontal tunnel. The tunnel traveled nearly 220 feet underground to the cave

WATER TUNNEL OF MEGIDDO

in which a spring — the city's water source — was located. One crew began digging in the cave, the other at the bottom of the shaft inside the city. When the builders met in the middle, they had accomplished one of the great engineering feats of the time! The cave where the spring was located was then sealed from the outside, securing the water supply from enemy attack. Every day women descended the steps that wound around the outside walls of the shaft and walked through the tunnel to the spring in order to draw water.

ANCIENT WALL BLOCKING THE CAVE OF THE SPRING AT MEGIDDO (OUTSIDE VIEW)

3. Ancient people tended to think of their gods in terms of a specific place or a specific aspect of life. That's why people who were fishermen tended to worship gods of the sea, people who lived near a volcano tended to worship gods of fire, and people who raised crops tended to worship gods of fertility or rain. So it is not surprising that the Canaanites attributed the fertility of their crops to their god, Baal. Discuss how the common perceptions ancient people had about their deities might have influenced or challenged how the Israelites thought about God when they began living in the Promised Land. What questions might they have had about their security and future when they worshiped a God who had faithfully fed, watered, and led them through the desert wilderness, but now they found themselves living

among people who settled in cities and depended more on
their crops than on their flocks for survival?

Faith Lesson (3 minutes)

When the Israelites moved into the Promised Land, an intense spiritual battle began for the hearts and minds of God's people. Again
and again we read about the Israelites' attraction to and worship of
Canaanite gods, God's disciplinary response, the people's repentance, and God's merciful forgiveness. But by the time of Ahab
and Jezebel, it seemed as if the battle had been lost; the worship
practices of the Canaanite fertility cults had the official sanction of
Israel's leaders. Yet prophets such as Elijah, Hosea, Isaiah, and Jeremiah continued to thunder that Yahweh was God and that he alone
deserved the people's allegiance. It took the destruction of Israel by
the Assyrians and the Babylonian captivity of Judah to convince the
Israelites that there is only one God.

It's easy for us to be critical of how the Israelites wavered in their
faithfulness to worship God and God alone. We're shocked by the
sins of child sacrifice and temple prostitution. Yet each of us partici-
pates in the same battle for total commitment to God. We may not
think of ourselves as idol worshipers, and we may not sacrifice our
children in order to have a good harvest, yet in every area of life we
still struggle to serve God completely.

1.   Which sinful patterns of belief and/or behavior are you hold-
     ing on to that prevent you from serving God completely?

2. What might you be sacrificing today in order to gain per-
    sonal security and success?

Closing (1 minute)

Read the following Scripture passage aloud, then pray, asking God to
make you aware of sin in your life and its consequences. Ask God to
give you the steadfast will to devote yourself completely to him and
to obey his Word so you can stand firmly against the gods of this
world.

Memorize

> *See, I am setting before you today a blessing and a curse—the blessing if you
> obey the commands of the LORD your God that I am giving you today; the
> curse if you disobey the commands of the LORD your God and turn from the
> way that I command you today by following other gods, which you have not
> known.*
>
> **Deuteronomy 11:26–28**

The Battle for Our Hearts, Minds, and Souls

In-Depth Personal Study Sessions

Day One | Living among the Gods of the Canaanites

The Very Words of God

> *I am the LORD your God, who brought you out of Egypt, out of the land of slavery. You shall have no other gods before me.*
>
> **Deuteronomy 5:6 – 7**

Bible Discovery

Canaanite Worship Practices

The people of Israel were called to worship and obey God so that all the world would know that Yahweh was the one true God. Yet God established their homeland in Canaan where the prevailing religions could be categorized as fertility cults. In addition to seeking to appease the gods through sacrifices (sometimes human), the Canaanites practiced many types of sexual perversion as part of their worship of Baal and Asherah (Ashtoreth).

1. Notice what the following verses reveal about the practices involved in the worship of Canaanite gods. What were these practices, and why were they offensive to God?

Scripture Text	Canaanite Worship Practices	Why the Practice Was Offensive to God
Deut. 7:4 – 5		

Deut. 18:9–14		
Deut. 23:17–18		
1 Kings 14:23–24		
2 Kings 21:2–9		

2. What do you think it must have been like to live for God in a culture where such practices were considered perfectly normal?

Reflection

Long before the Israelites entered Canaan, God warned his people about the dangerous religious practices that awaited them and instructed them not to participate in any way:

> When you enter the land the LORD your God is giving you, do not learn to imitate the detestable ways of the nations there. Let no one be found among you who sacrifices his son or daughter in the fire, who practices divination or sorcery, interprets omens, engages in witchcraft, or casts spells, or who is a medium or spiritist or who consults the dead. Anyone who does these things is detestable to the LORD.... You must be blameless before the LORD your God.
>
> **Deuteronomy 18:9–13**

What do you think happened that allowed the Israelites to participate in evil worship practices when God so clearly forbade them?

As you consider the Canaanites' worship practices, what similar practices are surfacing in our culture today (even though they may not be as "mainstream" as they were in the Canaanite culture)?

To what extent do we Christians (and you personally) tend to be sloppy about living blamelessly before God and put ourselves at risk for being drawn into practices that are detestable to him?

DATA FILE
The Gods of Canaan
Baal

The earliest deity recognized by people of the ancient Near East was the creator-god, El. His mistress, the fertility goddess Asherah, supposedly gave birth to many gods, including a powerful one named Baal ("Lord"). There appears to have been only one Baal who was manifested in lesser Baals at different times and places. Over time, Baal became the dominant deity and the worship of El faded away.

Baal is portrayed as a man with the head and horns of a bull, an image that is similar to that described in biblical accounts. His right hand (and sometimes both hands) was raised, and he held a lightning bolt that signified destruction and fertility. Baal was sometimes seated on a throne, possibly to show that he was the king or lord of the gods. He supposedly won his dominance by defeating other deities, including the god of the sea, the god of storms (also of rain, thunder, and lightning), and the god of death. His victory over death was thought to be repeated each year when he returned from the land of death (the underworld) and brought rain to renew the earth's fertility.

Hebrew culture viewed the sea as evil and destructive, so Baal's promise to prevent storms and control the sea, as well as his seeming ability to produce abundant harvests, made him attractive to the Israelites. It's difficult to understand why Yahweh's people failed to see that God alone had power over these things. Possibly their desert experience led them to question God's sovereignty over fertile land. Or perhaps the carnal appeal of some of the Canaanite worship practices attracted them to Baal.

Baal's worshipers appeased him by offering sacrifices, usually sheep and bulls (1 Kings 18:25–29). Some scholars believe that the Canaanites also sacrificed pigs and that God prohibited his people from eating pork in part to prevent this cult from being established among them. (See Isaiah 65:1–5 for an example of Israel's participation in the Canaanites' pagan practices.)

BAAL SACRIFICIAL ALTAR

continued on next page . . .

During times of crisis, however, Baal's followers offered more than animals. They sacrificed their children, apparently the firstborn of the community, in order to gain personal prosperity. The Bible calls this practice "detestable" (Deuteronomy 12:31; 18:9–10). God specifically appointed the tribe of Levi to be his special servants, in place of the firstborn of the Israelites, so they had no excuse for offering their children (Numbers 3:11–13). God hated child sacrifice, especially among those whom he had called to be his people.

Asherah

Asherah, in various forms and with varying names (Ashtoreth, for example), was honored as the fertility goddess (Judges 3:7). The Bible does not actually describe her, but archaeologists have discovered figurines believed to be representations of her. She is portrayed as a nude female, sometimes pregnant, with exaggerated breasts that she holds out apparently as symbols of her fertility. The Bible indicates that she was worshiped near trees and poles, called Asherah poles (Deuteronomy 7:5; 12:2–3; 2 Kings 16:4; 17:10; Jeremiah 3:6, 13; Ezekiel 6:13). Although Asherah was believed to be Baal's mother, she was also his mistress, and ritual sex was one way she was worshiped.

GODDESS ASHERAH

The Canaanites (as well as people of other pagan cultures) believed they could influence the gods' actions by performing the behavior they wished the gods to demonstrate. So, because they believed the sexual union of Baal and Asherah produced fertility, worshipers engaged in immoral sex in an effort to cause the gods to join together and thereby ensure good harvests. This practice became the basis for religious prostitution (1 Kings 14:23 – 24). The priest or a male community member represented Baal and the priestess or a female community member represented Asherah. Thus, God's incredible gift of sexuality within the bonds of marriage was perverted and became obscene public prostitution. No wonder God's anger burned against his people and their leaders when they participated in these practices.

Day Two | Israel's Descent into Baal Worship

The Very Words of God

> *You have forsaken me and served other gods, so I will no longer save you. Go and cry out to the gods you have chosen. Let them save you when you are in trouble!*

Judges 10:13 – 14

Bible Discovery

Progression into Paganism

From the time they started on their journey to the Promised Land, Israel dabbled in the worship practices of the pagan people around them. Once they began living in the land of the Canaanites, they began a rollercoaster-like descent into Baal worship. For short periods of time they were persuaded to worship and obey God, but they would soon turn away from God and return to the horrific practices of the pagans around them. This is not a short study, but it will open your eyes to God's view of pagan practices and the long-term consequences — individually and culturally — of disobedience to God.

1. Which Canaanite practices did God specifically forbid, and why? (See Leviticus 18:1 - 24, 29 - 30; 20:1 - 8.)

2. When did the Israelites first start imitating the worship practices of the people around them, and what was the result? (See Exodus 32:1 - 8.)

3. How far had the Israelites strayed from God and descended into the worship of Baal during the time of the judges? (See Judges 6:25 - 31.)

4. After the twelve tribes of Israel split into the nations of Israel and Judah, what did King Jeroboam of Israel do to solidify his political position? (See 1 Kings 12:26 - 33; 13:33 - 34.)

   What impact did his actions have on how the people worshiped?

How did God respond? (See 1 Kings 14:7 – 11.)

5. What was King Ahab's role in promoting Baal worship in Israel? (See 1 Kings 16:29 – 33.)

   How did King Ahab's example affect the hearts and minds of God's people? (See 1 Kings 18:16 – 24, especially verse 21.)

6. What eventually resulted from Israel's worship of Baal? (See 2 Kings 17:7 – 11, 15 – 19.)

7. For the most part, the kings and people of Judah also did not remain faithful in worshiping God. In what detestable worship practices did King Ahaz participate? (See 2 Kings 16:1 – 4.)

What did the kings and people of Judah have the audacity to do? (See 2 Kings 21:1 - 9; 23:4 - 7, 11 - 12.) NOTE: Some of these passages reveal what the people and kings of Judah had done by describing what King Josiah destroyed in order to eliminate pagan worship.

8. What eventually resulted from Judah's pagan practices? (See 2 Kings 23:26 - 27; 24:1 - 4, 13 - 14.)

Reflection

Israel's and Judah's continual disregard for God's commands and their subsequent descent into paganism are sobering. Their story gives us, as God-fearing believers, cause to reexamine our commitment to obey God and live for him and him alone.

To what degree do you see your culture assuming pagan values, much as ancient Israel did, and what impact does that have on you?

What departure from obedience to God and subsequent progression into evil have you seen —
    In your life?

In the life of a close friend or family member?

In the culture in which you live?

In which areas of your life do you need to strengthen your commitment to obey God and restore his values to their proper place in your life?

Memorize

God did not call us to be impure, but to live a holy life.

1 Thessalonians 4:7

Day Three | God Responds to the Evil Actions of His People

The Very Words of God

You have done more evil than all who lived before you. You have made for yourself other gods, idols made of metal; you have provoked me to anger and thrust me behind your back.

1 Kings 14:9

Bible Discovery

God's Response to Unfaithfulness

It's hard to imagine how entrenched Baal worship became among
God's people during Israel's history. Knowing that they would face
powerful, seductive temptations to think and act in evil ways in
the land he had given to them, God had called his people to remain
faithful to him. He had promised abundant blessings if the people
obeyed him. Instead of influencing their culture by holy living,
however, the Israelites often turned away from God to pursue the
worship of Baal and other gods. God hated their evil practices, especially the shedding of innocent blood. He had to take action.

1. Even before the Israelites crossed the Jordan River and
   entered the Promised Land, some of them had begun to worship Canaanite gods. (See Numbers 25:1 – 13.)

   a. How did God respond to their disobedience?

   b. What do you learn from this account about how impor-
      tant obedience is to God?

2. Judges 10:6 – 16 relates another account of Israel's abandon-
   ment of God in favor of pagan gods.

   a. Which gods did Israel worship, and how did God
      respond to their unfaithfulness?

   b. What does this story reveal to you about how much God
      loves his people and how he responds to repentance?

3. King Solomon, Israel's wisest and most influential king, was seduced into worshiping the gods of his foreign wives. (See 1 Kings 10:23 - 24; 11:1 - 13.)

   a. Notice how close to God Solomon had been early in his life. Why did he turn away from God?

   b. What do you learn from God's response to Solomon's unfaithfulness about how seriously God considers disobedience and how committed he is to honoring those who follow him faithfully?

4. In 2 Chronicles 33:1 - 13 we read about God's interaction with and response to the evil of King Manasseh and the people of Judah.

   a. What did God do when Manasseh and his people paid no attention to him?

   b. What do you learn from this story about the depth of God's love and forgiveness?

   c. Is this how you would have expected God to respond? Why or why not?

Reflection

God will not close his eyes to the sin of his people. He cannot ignore detestable acts, and he will not stand for the shedding of innocent blood. The adulterous pursuit of other gods and reckless indulgence in sin provoke him to anger. Yet in Jeremiah 15:19, we read an amazing promise that reveals the heart and character of God: "If you repent, I will restore you that you may serve me." When those who have sinned against God turn away from their sin and choose to obey him faithfully, God is merciful and generous with his forgiveness.

Why do you think God takes the unfaithfulness of his people so seriously?

When those of us who are Christians choose to disobey God repeatedly, what are we revealing about ourselves?

What are we saying to God?

What are we communicating about God and his Word to those around us?

Which practices or attitudes in your life may provoke God to anger?

What must God do to get *your* attention so that you will turn your heart completely toward him?

Day Four | Mixing Righteousness with Evil

The Very Words of God

> He [the LORD] has showed you, O man, what is good. And what does the LORD require of you? To act justly and to love mercy and to walk humbly with your God.
>
> **Micah 6:8**

Bible Discovery

We Cannot Honor God While Participating in Evil

God called the Israelites to serve him and him alone, but they often wavered between the two: first serving God, then sacrificing to other gods, and sometimes worshiping both. During King Ahab's reign, for example, while the Israelites claimed to worship God they also worshiped Canaanite gods, sacrificed their children for personal gain, burned incense under Asherah poles, and participated in ritual prostitution. God strongly condemned their claim to honor him while they engaged in such abominable practices.

1. The words of the Lord in Jeremiah 7:1 – 20 convey a powerful message to anyone who thinks it is acceptable to worship God one moment and to participate in evil the next moment.

    a. Which attitude(s) and/or action(s) did God single out as being particularly detestable?

b. In what specific ways were the Israelites to demonstrate their commitment to turn back to God and serve him? How did these actions differ from what the Israelites practiced when they worshiped Baal?

c. How great was God's anger against the unfaithfulness of his people?

d. What was at stake if the people did not turn back to God?

2. God sent Ezekiel to warn God's people of the consequences of their sins: their lewd immorality, their sacrifice of their children, and their desecration of his temple. (See Ezekiel 23:1 - 7, 11 - 13, 36 - 39, 48 - 49.) NOTE: Oholah and Oholibah are names for Israel and Judah.

a. How do you think God's people justified sacrificing their children and then entering God's temple to worship him?

b. Why was God going to make his people suffer the consequences of their idolatry? (See verses 48 - 49.)

Reflection

When Elijah confronted the prophets of Baal (1 Kings 18:20 – 24ff), he asked the people a crucial question: "How long will you waver between two opinions?" The people apparently weren't convinced that God was truly God, so they worshiped whichever gods they pleased in whatever ways pleased them. That is not the kind of worship our sovereign Lord requires.

In what ways do we as Christians today "waver between two opinions" when it comes to our daily life and worship of God?

What are some of the specific compromises we make with evil in our world, and how do these compromises affect our walk with God, our relationships with our family, and our influence at work and in our communities?

How deep is your loyalty to God in the battle between good and evil, and in what ways do you demonstrate your faithfulness to him in the battle for the hearts, minds, and souls of people?

Memorize

Let us throw off everything that hinders and the sin that so easily entangles, and let us run with perseverance the race marked out for us.

Hebrews 12:1

Day Five | God Has His Limits

The Very Words of God

> O LORD, do not your eyes look for truth? You struck them, but they felt no
> pain; you crushed them, but they refused correction. They made their faces
> harder than stone and refused to repent.

Jeremiah 5:3

Bible Discovery

When God's Judgment Falls

God exercises great patience in his love for his people. Sometimes,
however, he cannot tolerate any more of their sin and brings judgment — as he did against the Israelites who persisted in evil and
spilled innocent blood. The following review of Israel's history will
show how God responded to the faithful and unfaithful kings of his
people after their nation split into two parts — Israel (the ten northern tribes) and Judah.

King/Scripture Text	Actions of the King/ the People	God's Response
Hoshea of Israel 2 Kings 17:1–6, 9–18		
Hezekiah of Judah 2 Kings 18:1–18; 2 Chron. 31:1		
Manasseh, Hezekiah's son 2 Chron. 33:1–6, 9–17		

Amon, Hezekiah's grandson 2 Chron. 33:21–25		
Josiah, Hezekiah's great-grandson 2 Chron. 34:1–8, 30–33; 35:25–27		
Zedekiah 2 Chron. 36:11–20		

Reflection

The day eventually came when God said to his prophet Jeremiah, "This is the nation that has not obeyed the LORD its God or responded to correction. Truth has perished; it has vanished from their lips ... take up a lament on the barren heights, for the LORD has rejected and abandoned this generation that is under his wrath" (Jeremiah 7:28-29).

Take some time to consider your life, the life of God's people in your church, your community, and your nation.

In what ways are you and God's people responding to God's correction and serving him faithfully?

In what ways might God consider you to be part of an unfaithful and disobedient generation?

How far will you go to demonstrate your loyalty to the one true God by obeying and serving him alone so that all the world will know that he is God?

INNOCENT BLOOD – PART TWO

This session will complete the study we began in session one. We will once again focus our attention on faith lessons from Tel Megiddo, the remains of an important city in ancient Israel. We will continue to explore the far-reaching impact of the Israelites' worship of Canaanite gods and consider our role in influencing the Megiddos of our day. The DVD segment for this session features highlights from the "Innocent Blood" segment viewed previously. It will serve as a review for participants who saw the DVD segment for session one and will provide participants who missed that session with sufficient background to fully participate in this session.

In ancient times, the great city of Megiddo towered above the Plain of Jezreel and the Via Maris. Because of its location, the city was a strategic focal point for economic and political control of the ancient world. Megiddo was also a highly visible place where God's people had the opportunity to engage in the ongoing battle between good and evil and exert his influence on world culture. So this session emphasizes the significance of Megiddo as a stronghold in the spiritual battle for control of the hearts, minds, and souls of God's people.

As Christians today, we also are participants in the battle for spiritual control represented by Megiddo. In this session, we are challenged to exert influence on the "Megiddos" of our world — the strategic places where culture can be influenced — be they Hollywood, Wall Street, Washington, D.C., or our own neighborhoods and families.

The ongoing battle between good and evil has great consequences. People who stand firmly for God, who resist the sinful and seductive influences of culture, and who advocate God's principles in an increasingly pagan world are fighting a battle that will continue until the world's end. Despite the difficulties in fighting this battle, God's people can take heart. Jesus grew up in Nazareth, within sight of Megiddo, and lived there until he began his public ministry. How often he must have looked at Megiddo, knowing what had happened there, what it represented during his day, and what it would stand for in the future. You see, the word *Armageddon*, the final battle between good and evil, is derived from the Hebrew word *Har* (meaning "hill," "mound," or "mount") and *Megiddon* (meaning Megiddo). So in a sense, the work of Jesus began at Armageddon and will one day end at Armageddon when his victory over evil is complete.

Opening Thoughts (4 minutes)

The Very Words of God

> Now fear the LORD and serve him with all faithfulness. Throw away the gods your forefathers worshiped beyond the River and in Egypt, and serve the LORD. But if serving the LORD seems undesirable to you, then choose for yourselves this day whom you will serve.... But as for me and my household, we will serve the LORD.
>
> Joshua 24:14–15

Think About It

Many of us want to be considered "successful" in life and will sacrifice much in order to gain personal status. Yet our efforts to achieve success may harm innocent people and have long-term impact on the battle between good and evil.

How do you think a historian 150 years from now might describe the values and priorities of our culture? How might that historian evaluate what we are willing to sacrifice for success and what our impact is with respect to the battle between good and evil?

DVD Teaching Notes (17 minutes)

Tel Megiddo: strategic point for world control

Baal vs. God: the battle for spiritual control

The consequences of our choices

God's response to evil

DVD Discussion (7 minutes)

1. Take a moment to consider the geographical features of the
   map of the Valley of Jezreel. Notice the location of the Jezreel Valley, the proximity of Nazareth and Megiddo — just
   ten miles apart — on opposite sides of the valley, and the
   route of the Via Maris. Why was it important for God's
   people to occupy such an influential city as Megiddo?

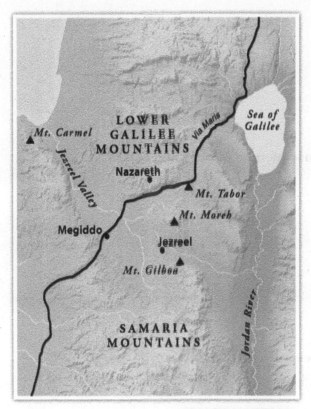

VALLEY OF JEZREEL

2.　What are the spiritual battles of "Megiddo" really about, and what is at stake in these battles?

As you consider the battles for good and evil taking place in our culture, which short- and long-term consequences can you identify?

VALLEY OF JEZREEL VIEWED ACROSS THE ALTAR AT MEGIDDO

3. When we find ourselves at a difficult place in the battle between good and evil, even when it seems that evil has the upper hand, what enduring hope does Megiddo represent?

HOW IMPORTANT ARE THE BATTLES OF MEGIDDO?

Megiddo is a *tel*, a mound composed of layers (or strata) of civilizations, and each layer provides a record of the people who lived there. We know that Megiddo was an important city during ancient times because of its large size and the great number of layers within it (more than twenty, some of which represent more than one settlement).

We also know that many battles were fought near Megiddo as opposing empires sought to control the city and the Via Maris trade route. In fact, some scholars believe more battles have been fought in the vicinity of Megiddo and the Jezreel Valley than at any other place in the world.

Megiddo also foreshadows a strategic battle in the future. The word *Armageddon*, the final battle between good and evil described in Revelation 16:16, is derived from the Hebrew word *Har* (meaning a "hill," "mound," or "mount") and *Megiddon* (meaning Megiddo). By choosing Megiddo to be the symbol of the end-times battle, the writer of Revelation revealed that the final battle of Armageddon will determine who will ultimately control the world. [NOTE: Some Christians believe the reference to Armageddon is symbolic; others believe that a literal battle for world domination will take place.]

Small Group Bible Discovery and Discussion (20 minutes)

Our Struggle to Influence the "Megiddos" of Culture

Megiddo stood guard over the Via Maris at a key mountain pass above the Valley of Jezreel. Whoever controlled this strategic city controlled the trade route. Today, Megiddo still represents a strategic control point. As was true in ancient Israel, great spiritual battles are taking place between people who follow God and people who follow the gods of this world, between the values of God and the values of Satan. These battles are for the hearts, minds, and souls of people. The consequences are great—for us as individuals, for our families, for the church, and for our communities, country, and world.

1. Why does God want his people to actively participate in and exert influence on strategic points of cultural influence such as Megiddo? (See Isaiah 43:10-12.)

2. One of Satan's most successful methods for undermining God-honoring cultural values and seizing control of the hearts, minds, and souls of people has been through the perversion of God's gift of sexuality. Long before the Israelites entered the Promised Land, God knew that sexual practices related to the worship of Canaanite gods would lead his people astray.

   a. What commands did God give his people regarding their sexual behavior? (See Exodus 20:14; Leviticus 18:6-23.)

    b. Why was obedience to these commands important to God? (See Leviticus 18:1 - 5; 20:7, 22 - 24.)

3. What kind of a culture do you think God wanted his people to demonstrate to the world by following his commands for purity in their sexual relationships and in their relationship with him?

   In what ways do you think daily life in such a culture would have differed from the everyday life to which the Canaanites were accustomed?

   When God's people became just like the Canaanites, what happened to their ability to influence others for God?

4. Our sexual behavior is just one example of how God's people can influence culture for good or for evil. Why do you think this video emphasized the need for Christians to occupy other prominent "Megiddos" of our culture (Hollywood, Wall Street, Washington, D.C., our families)?

What battles for good or evil are being fought in these arenas, and what might be the consequences of these battles?

To what extent do you think Christians today seem to have surrendered the "Megiddos" of culture to those who follow the gods of this world?

Faith Lesson (6 minutes)

God calls us to participate in the battles between good and evil in order to influence the "Megiddos" of our culture in strategic ways so they will reflect more of God and his values. Just as Megiddo played a key role in ancient Israel, so we are called to influence strategic areas within our culture and share the values of God—through our attitudes, words, and actions.

1. Where is your allegiance in the battle between good and evil, and how deep is your loyalty?

2. To what extent do you expend yourself to influence the "Megiddos" of your world—the media, government, community leaders, neighbors, educators, etc.—by exhibiting the values of God?

3. Where is your "Megiddo," the center of influence where God has placed you? What has God called you to accomplish there?

4. Can you identify another "Megiddo" — perhaps a more powerful center of influence — that God might be preparing you to influence for him in the future?

Closing (1 minute)

Read Matthew 5:14 - 16 aloud: "You are the light of the world. A city on a hill cannot be hidden. Neither do people light a lamp and put it under a bowl. Instead they put it on its stand, and it gives light to everyone in the house. In the same way, let your light shine before men, that they may see your good deeds and praise your Father in heaven."

Then ask God to use this session and your time of personal study to help you be a bright, shining light that reveals his character and values in your world. Ask him to give you a heart that is committed to being faithful to him in every way.

Memorize

You are the light of the world.... Let your light shine before men, that they may see your good deeds and praise your Father in heaven.

Matthew 5:14, 16

The Battle for Our Hearts, Minds, and Souls

In-Depth Personal Study Sessions

Day One Identifying the Gods of
Our Culture

The Very Words of God

> *Grace and peace to you from God our Father and the Lord Jesus Christ, who gave himself for our sins to rescue us from the present evil age, according to the will of our God and Father, to whom be glory for ever and ever. Amen.*
>
> **Galatians 1:3 – 5**

Bible Discovery

Which Gods Do We Worship?

Most people in our culture don't worship man-made idols or have altars to various gods in their homes, and it would be difficult to find a neighborhood Asherah pole in suburban America. Satan is still very good, however, at enticing us to worship other gods. Take a few minutes to explore what the Bible reveals about these attractive and seductive gods; then consider the ways in which these gods are evident today.

THINK ABOUT IT
How Much Has Really Changed?
Canaan's fertility cults and practices have numerous parallels to our day. For example, cultures throughout the world demonstrate a growing disregard for the sacredness of human life. In some cultures, human life is terminated for personal convenience; in others it is terminated for economic, social, or political gain. Sexuality, too, has become the goddess of much of Western

continued on next page . . .

society. It is promoted in the arts, media, music, and advertising — as if genuine success in life depends on a beautiful appearance or sexual prowess.

When it comes to pursuing the gods of this world, human beings haven't changed all that much in three thousand years. Nor has God. He still detests our pursuit of other gods. He is appalled by the ways we devalue human life, whether that occurs through abortion, oppression, ethnic cleansing, or euthanasia. He abhors the ways in which we have perverted his gift of sexuality.

As Christians, we are called to obey God's laws concerning sexuality and the sacredness of human life. We are also called to prophetically address the sinfulness of our culture and to demonstrate by example that obeying God's laws leads to true fulfillment. What does fulfillment of this calling require us to do? What does it look like to defend the innocent, to give relief to the oppressed, and to live with a pure heart in the midst of evil so that our world will see that God is the one true God?

1. As you read the following passages, write down what you discover about the "gods" that can lead us away from worshiping and obeying God with all our heart, soul, and strength.

Scripture Text	Identify the God(s) Mentioned in the Text	God's Response
Dan. 4:27–37		
Matt. 20:20–28		
Luke 16:13–15		

2 Tim. 3:1–4		
James 3:13–16		
1 John 2:15–17		

2. When we take a close look at the gods that have led God's people astray in the past, it can be a bit easier for us to see the idols in our own culture that lure us away from worshiping and obeying God.

   a. What makes our pursuit of the gods of culture so insidious?

   b. Which of the gods mentioned above are you most easily enticed to pursue?

   c. Why are these particular gods difficult for you to deal with?

Reflection

While Jesus was on earth, Satan even tried to seduce him to use his power to gain earthly kingdoms. But Jesus was not fooled; he knew exactly what was at stake and responded with great clarity, "It is written: 'Worship the Lord your God and serve him only'" (Luke 4:8).

> Chances are, you have been seduced to follow at least some of the gods of this world. How has pursuing these gods affected your relationship with God and influenced the lives of others?

> When life presents so many attractive alternatives, how does Jesus' response help you stand firm in your commitment to turn away from the gods of this world and worship God alone?

Memorize

Jesus answered, "It is written: 'Worship the Lord your God and serve him only.'"

Luke 4:8

Day Two | Resisting the Gods of This World

The Very Words of God

Your enemy the devil prowls around like a roaring lion looking for someone to devour. Resist him, standing firm in the faith.

1 Peter 5:8–9

Bible Discovery

A Strategy for Resistance

God calls us to worship him — and him alone — not wealth, fame, or any other popular gods of culture. But how can we do this when our culture surrounds us with inviting opportunities and enticing images that seem so convenient, harmless — and "normal"? How do we learn to resist? One way is by pursuing God. The following exploration will help you discover how King David, whom God called "a man after my own heart" (Acts 13:22), resisted the gods of this world.

1. What desires did David express in Psalms 51:10 - 12 and 139:23 - 24?

    How would similar desires help you resist the lure of the gods of this world?

2. Read Psalms 1:1 - 3 and 119:9 - 20, which highlight a number of practical ways to obey and honor God, and list the ways to keep one's heart pure before God. Then, describe how you would do these things in your life.

3. Prayer is essential for anyone who desires to follow God and resist Satan. What attitude did David have toward God when he prayed, and what did he pray about? (See Psalms 5:1 - 8; 25:4 - 5.)

In what ways is your prayer life similar to, or different from, David's?

What changes might you want to make so that your prayers become a more powerful force in resisting the gods of this world?

4. How committed was David to obeying God, and what did he do to keep his relationship with God vibrant? (See Psalms 26:2 - 3; 32:1 - 5.)

Reflection

We don't have to read many of David's psalms to realize that he had extraordinary trust in God's character and Word. David looked to God as his refuge, fortress, shield, and deliverer. He trusted in God's laws because he saw that they gave joy to the heart and light to the eyes. That trust helped him to resist the enticements that surrounded him. In Psalm 40:4 David wrote, "Blessed is the man who makes the LORD his trust, who does not look to the proud, to those who turn aside to false gods."

What are you afraid God will fail to provide that you hope to gain by turning to the false gods of this world?

What are you willing to do (such as the specific practices outlined in the Bible Discovery) in order to learn that God is completely faithful and trustworthy? In order to trust in God rather than depending on and pursuing the enticing gods of culture?

Memorize

Be on your guard; stand firm in the faith; be men of courage; be strong.

1 Corinthians 16:13

Day Three | Facing Our "Insignificant" Sins

The Very Words of God

Everyone who sins breaks the law; in fact, sin is lawlessness.

1 John 3:4

Bible Discovery

All Sin Is Serious

When we learn about the sins of ancient Israel as they abandoned God to worship the gods of the surrounding cultures, it can be all too easy for us to think, *What they did sure was blatant ... the shrine prostitutes, the idols, the child sacrifices. I'd never do things like that. My sins are small in comparison; they aren't going to have much of an impact.* But consider what God says about our so-called "little sins."

1. When God placed his people in the Promised Land, he commanded them to love him with their whole heart, soul, and strength—to worship him exclusively and obey him completely. (See Deuteronomy 6:1 - 25.) God also has set standards for those of us who call ourselves Christians.

   a. Although they may be expressed a bit differently from the commands Moses gave to the Israelites, what are God's standards for his people and what do they require of us? (See Matthew 22:37 - 40; Romans 12:1 - 2; 1 Corinthians 6:19; 10:31 - 33; 1 Thessalonians 5:16 - 23; Titus 2:11 - 13; 1 John 2:5 - 6; 3:8 - 10.)

   b. According to these standards, what room is there for sin in the hearts and lives of God's people?

2. Although we may like to think that some of our sins are insignificant and not troublesome enough to deal with, God has a different perspective. (See Job 34:21 - 22; Psalms 44:20; 94:11; Isaiah 29:15.)

   a. What do you learn from these passages about how seriously God views our sins?

    b. In what ways do these passages change your perspective on your sins?

3. What strong language is used in Colossians 3:1 – 10 to describe how a Christian must deal with sin in his or her life?

    Why is such strong treatment of *all* sin — what we might label as both "large" and "small" sins — necessary?

    Consider for a moment the path Israel followed into Baal worship. What might be the long-term consequences in your life if you choose to overlook certain "little" sins?

4. In addition to putting to death our sinful nature, what are we, as God's chosen people, to put on every day as we go through life? (See Colossians 3:12 – 17.) How will doing this influence our culture for God?

THINK ABOUT IT

Unconfessed sin is powerful. Consider just a few examples of the results of sin:

- Sin can cause God to stop listening to our prayers. (See Psalm 66:18–19; Isaiah 59:1–3.)
- Sin can be troubling to us. (See Psalm 38:18.)
- Sin can lead to rebuke and discipline from God. (See Psalm 39:11.)
- Sin may be attractive, but it leads to death. (See Romans 6:23; James 1:15.)
- Sin can cause God to hide his face from us. (See Isaiah 64:7.)
- Everyone who sins is a slave to sin. (See John 8:34.)

Reflection

In Psalm 19:12 - 14, David wrote:

> *Forgive my hidden faults.*
> *Keep your servant also from willful sins;*
>   *may they not rule over me.*
> *Then will I be blameless,*
>   *innocent of great transgression.*
> *May the words of my mouth and the meditation of my heart*
>   *be pleasing in your sight,*
>   *O LORD, my Rock and my Redeemer.*

What are some of your "hidden faults" or "willful sins"?

In what ways do these unconfessed sins damage your relationship with God and undermine your influence for him in the world?

If you were to take your sins as seriously as God does, how might you need to think differently? What might you need to do differently?

What practical steps will you take to have a pure heart before God and honor him in everything you think, say, and do?

Day Four | Who Will Walk with God?

The Very Words of God

> *Josiah was eight years old when he became king.... He did what was right in the eyes of the LORD and walked in all the ways of his father David, not turning aside to the right or to the left.*
>
> *2 Kings 22:1 – 2*

Bible Discovery

What Legacy of Faith Will We Pass On?

Throughout their history, the ancient Israelites had an "off again, on again" relationship with God. Even though he had chosen them to be his holy people and to influence the world for him, they often chose to pursue false gods. Sometimes godly leaders such as King Hezekiah and King Josiah stepped into the gap and led the people back to God. Explore for a moment what took place before, during, and after their respective reigns and consider the parallels to our lives and the spiritual legacy we are leaving behind.

1. Because Israel (the ten northern tribes) persisted in their worship of Baal and the pursuit of all that God had forbid-

den them to do, what happened during King Hoshea's reign?
(See 2 Kings 17:14 - 18, 22 = 23.)

2. In order to prevent a similar disaster from happening to
   Judah, what did King Hezekiah do? (See 2 Chronicles 31:1,
   20 - 21.)

   What happened to Judah as a result, and what influence did
   Hezekiah's reign have on the people of Judah? (See 2 Chronicles 32:1, 9 - 23.)

3. Despite the God-fearing spiritual legacy of Hezekiah, which
   spiritual path did his son, Manasseh, choose? (See 2 Chronicles 33:1 - 6.)

   What did God do to get Manasseh's attention, and what was
   the result? (See 2 Chronicles 33:10 - 13, 15 - 16.)

Which part of his father's spiritual legacy did Hezekiah's grandson, Amon, choose to follow? (See 2 Chronicles 33:21 – 23.)

4. What do you think led Manasseh and Amon to follow the spiritual paths they chose when Hezekiah had been such a strong example of faithful obedience to God?

What are the implications for those of us who desire to pass our faith to the next generation?

5. Josiah, Hezekiah's great-grandson, was a godly king. What things did he do to bring Judah back to faithful obedience to God and to leave a legacy of faithfulness to God? (See 2 Chronicles 34:1 – 8, 14, 19 – 33.)

HOW LONG DID IT LAST?

After King Josiah's death, God's people once again steadfastly worshiped false gods. As he had promised, God did not allow disaster to fall on Judah during Josiah's reign. But just twenty-three years after Josiah died, the Babylonian army destroyed the temple in Jerusalem and took the remaining Jews into captivity (2 Chronicles 36:15 – 20).

Reflection

Despite all he had done to obey God and to bring Judah back to worshiping God, in 609 BC King Josiah disobeyed God's command and went to fight Neco, King of Egypt, on the plain of Megiddo (the Jezreel Valley). Josiah was killed because of his disobedience, and his death had a tremendous impact on God's people. Just a few months after Josiah died, the battle between good and evil that had waged throughout Israel's history took its final turn toward evil. Judah pursued the evil practices of the Canaanites until the kings of Judah were no more. (See 2 Chronicles 35:20–24; 36:1–20.)

Why is it important to steadfastly obey God throughout all of life?

What do you think happens in the hearts of God's people when a godly leader openly disobeys God?

What steps are you taking to ensure that you will be faithful to the very end?

Who in your world do you consider to be a "Hezekiah" or "Josiah" who walks with God and confronts evil? In what ways might God be calling you to be such a person?

Memorize

> *Be careful to do what the* LORD *your God has commanded you; do not turn aside to the right or to the left. Walk in all the way that the* LORD *your God has commanded you, so that you may live and prosper and prolong your days in the land that you will possess.*
>
> *Deuteronomy 5:32–33*

Day Five | Megiddo: A Symbol of Hope and Promise

The Very Words of God

> *They will make war against the Lamb, but the Lamb will overcome them because he is Lord of lords and King of kings — and with him will be his called, chosen and faithful followers.*
>
> *Revelation 17:14*

Bible Discovery

Evil Will Not Prevail

The ancient city of Megiddo reminds us that the spiritual battle between good and evil is ultimately the battle for control of the world. Because of the redemptive work of Jesus Christ, those who stand with him and engage in the fight against evil can take heart. When the battle is finally over, Christ, the Lord of lords and King of kings, will be the victor.

1. Megiddo stands as a reminder of the ongoing battle between good and evil — the battle to influence culture for God or for Satan. It is interesting that Jesus grew up within sight of the Valley of Jezreel and Megiddo. What must he have thought as he looked over that valley? What are your thoughts as you consider what has happened and will happen there?

What does the "high place" at Megiddo, where Baal was worshiped, represent in ancient Israel's battle against evil?

What event took place in the valley of Megiddo that turned the tide of the battle for Judah? (See 2 Kings 23:29 – 32.)

Why is it significant that the Jewish author of Revelation located the most decisive battle of the ages at Megiddo? (See Revelation 16:12 – 16.)

2. Why did Jesus — God's Son, the promised Messiah — come to earth, and what did he accomplish for us? (See 1 Timothy 2:5 – 6; 1 John 3:8.)

3. Jesus also lived among us, where he could impact his culture. How effectively did he show the world that the God of Israel is the one true God? (See Matthew 15:29 – 31.)

4. Where is Jesus right now, and what is and will be his position when the final battle between good and evil is over? (See 1 Peter 3:21 – 22; Revelation 5:12 – 13; 17:14.)

5. Since the garden of Eden, Satan has delighted in drawing God's people to worship false gods and to sin against God. Despite his victories in the battle between good and evil, what will his ultimate fate be? (See John 12:31; Revelation 20:1-3, 7-10.)

Reflection

After the death and resurrection of Jesus, his followers were keenly aware of their role in the battle between good and evil. Paul wrote, "I have fought the good fight, I have finished the race, I have kept the faith. Now there is in store for me the crown of righteousness, which the Lord, the righteous Judge, will award to me on that day" (2 Timothy 4:7-8a). In a similar vein, James 1:12 says, "Blessed is the man who perseveres under trial, because when he has stood the test, he will receive the crown of life that God has promised to those who love him." These followers of Jesus knew their mission. They knew their hope. Against all odds, they went out and changed their world for God.

What is the certain hope of all Christians — all those who believe in Jesus Christ and have invited him to be their Lord and Savior?

It isn't easy to run the race to the finish or to fight the good fight. What intimidates you as you face the battle to influence culture — your Megiddo — for God?

Why is it important to remember, every day, that Jesus has already won the spiritual battle against Satan? What encouragement does this hope provide for your day-to-day life and the battle(s) you are fighting?

What are you doing today to stay engaged in the spiritual battle against evil? Which false gods and evil practices are you opposing for God?

THE EVIDENCE OF TIME
How to Tell a Tel

Israel is a land of hills and mountains. In fact, a first-time visitor often is amazed by how little flat land there is. Most travelers also notice that Israel is dotted with a distinctive type of hill that has steep sides, a flat top, and looks a bit like a coffee table—especially when it is located in a valley and is viewed from above. Such a hill is called a *tel*, and tels are particularly important to Bible students.

A tel comprises layers and layers of ruined settlements that have been rebuilt on top of the ruins of previous settlements. In general terms, here's how tels such as Tel Megiddo were formed.

Stage 1

People settled on the site, eventually building a wall and a gate. The king or rulers would build a palace and a temple, and the people would build houses inside the city walls. Often a steeply sloped rampart was built against the wall to protect the hill from erosion and to keep enemies away from the base of the wall. Over time, the ramparts were replaced or covered with others. These buried walls and ramparts gave the hill its steep, straight shape.

Stage 2

As the city grew and prospered, it became an attractive prize. Enemies would lay siege to it, sometimes penetrating the defenses and killing its inhabitants. Armies were usually brutally destructive in their conquests. Occasionally enemies remained to occupy the city, but usually they marched off, leaving behind smoking ruins.

Because of droughts, wars, or other reasons, once-prosperous cities were sometimes abandoned. Sand carried by the relentless winds of the region gradually covered what remained of the houses and streets. Nomads would pitch their tents on the site, then move on. Soon the ruins blended into the landscape.

Stage 3

Even when a city was destroyed or abandoned, the conditions necessary for establishing a settlement in that place usually remained—a water source or adequate rainfall, an occupation that could generate a consistent food supply, and a defensible location. So people eventually resettled on the abandoned site. Lacking heavy equipment to remove debris left by previous inhabitants, the newcomers filled in holes, leveled off the top of the hill, and rebuilt. Soon another prosperous community developed. Inevitably, its success attracted enemies ... and the cycle of destruction and rebuilding continued.

Stage 4

Over centuries—even millennia—layers upon layers of settlements accumulated (sort of like a layer cake), so the tel became higher and higher. Each layer, or stratum, records what life was like during the time of a particular settlement. Jerusalem has at least twenty-one layers, and Megiddo has

TEL BETH SHEAN

continued on next page ...

even more. Locked within these layers are artifacts such as pottery, jewelry, weapons, documents, gates, temples, palaces, and houses waiting to be uncovered by archaeologists so we can discover how the people of those settlements lived.

Artifacts unearthed at Tel Megiddo and other tels enable us to know how people lived during biblical times: what they ate, how they worshiped, what work they did, and many other important details. Each tel is, in effect, a unique gift from God that helps us learn more about life in ancient times so that we can better understand the Bible's message.

WHO IS GOD?

Although God had revealed himself and demonstrated his saving power to the Israelites over and over again, they were unwilling to live as God had called them to live. As time passed, they became increasingly confused about who God was and increasingly attracted to the Canaanite gods. By the time the prophet Elijah appeared, the Israelites had compromised their beliefs and values concerning God and were worshiping Baal. Even their king (Ahab) had married a Baal priestess from Phoenicia (Jezebel) and had done "more to provoke the LORD, the God of Israel, to anger than did all the kings of Israel before him" (1 Kings 16:33).

Israel's dalliance with Baal worship, which included indulgence in forbidden sexual practices and the sacrifice of children, had become a stumbling block to their role of bringing about God's plan of salvation. So God sent Elijah, the first of the great prophets, to turn the hearts of Israel back toward God. Today's session highlights a confrontation on the top of Mount Carmel between Elijah and 850 prophets of Baal and Asherah.

Elijah's encounter with the false prophets was strategic in both time and place. Mount Carmel, which literally means *God's vineyard*, receives about thirty inches of rain per year and overlooks the fertile Jezreel Valley — the breadbasket of ancient Israel. In Scripture, Mount Carmel symbolizes fertility and blessing, but because of Elijah's command there had been no rain or dew in Israel for more than three years (1 Kings 17:1)! In addition, the Via Maris — the trade route between the great empires of the ancient world — passed through the Jezreel Valley near Mount Carmel. Whatever happened on Mount Carmel would become widely known.

Although the Israelites worshiped Baal, they had not completely rejected the God of their fathers, so Elijah confronted them with

God's demand for total allegiance. He challenged them by saying, "How long will you waver between two opinions? If the LORD is God, follow him; but if Baal is God, follow him" (1 Kings 18:21). His challenge was similar to Joshua's challenge years earlier: "But if serving the LORD seems undesirable to you," Joshua had said, "then choose for yourselves this day whom you will serve" (Joshua 24:15). When Joshua posed his question, all of Israel chose to serve God. But when Elijah asked the people to choose, they said nothing!

Elijah gave the prophets of Baal the first opportunity to ask their god to burn up the offering of a bull — the sacred animal of Baal. Despite their frantic efforts, Baal didn't answer. So Elijah used twelve stones (one for each tribe of Israel) to repair the broken altar of the Lord that was there. He placed his bull upon it and, after dousing the sacrifice with water, called on God to answer him "so these people will know that you, O LORD, are God, and that you are turning their hearts back again" (1 Kings 18:37).

Immediately God sent down his fire! Lightning burned up the sacrifice, altar, water, and even the surrounding earth. The Israelites cried out, "Yahweh, he is God!" They had seen Elijah (whose name means *Yahweh is God*) in action and immediately recognized God. The Baal prophets were killed, Elijah prayed for rain, and God sent it. Although Israel eventually reverted to Baal worship, Elijah had done what God had called him to do, and at least for a moment the people recognized that Yahweh truly is God.

Opening Thoughts (4 minutes)

The Very Words of God

> *Elijah went before the people and said, "How long will you waver between two opinions? If the LORD is God, follow him; but if Baal is God, follow him." But the people said nothing.*
>
> 1 Kings 18:21

Think About It

At one time or another, all of us face some uncertainty regarding our faith in God. We may feel pulled between two opposing values and have a difficult time choosing one over the other, or we may waver in the strength of our commitment to live for God in every area of life.

What are some of the things that can lead us to lose faith in God and to pursue other "gods" that promise to make life better for us?

DVD Teaching Notes (21 minutes)

The geographical setting—Mount Carmel

The historical setting—King Ahab

Elijah—his name, his mission

The confrontation on Mount Carmel

DVD Discussion (7 minutes)

1. What things did King Ahab do that promoted the worship of Baal in Israel, and what was the effect of his leadership on the people?

2. Why is the meaning of Elijah's name (Yahweh is God) significant in light of his confrontations with King Ahab and Jezebel and with the prophets of Baal on Mount Carmel? What effect might his name have had on the people of Israel?

3. When we think of three and a half years without rain, we think of drought and hunger. What else might the Israelites, whose faith was wavering between God and Baal, have thought about when not a drop of moisture fell on their land?

Small Group Bible Discovery and Discussion (17 minutes)

How Do People Find Out That God Is God?

God reveals himself to people in many ways, such as through the splendor of his handiwork in nature, through the power of his Word, and sometimes through signs and miracles. People also discover who God is by observing the attitudes, actions, and words

of those who follow him. People are watching and listening, looking for signs of God at work. Often, what they see and hear greatly
affects their view of God and whether they choose to follow him.

1. How did God prove himself to Pharaoh and the Egyptians?
   (See Exodus 7:1 - 5.)

2. As the people of Israel marched toward the Promised Land,
   what did God do to reveal himself to "all the peoples of the
   earth"? (See Joshua 2:8 - 11; 4:19 - 24.)

   What effect did his mighty power have on Israel, and on the
   Canaanites?

   What effect does it have on you?

3. What did God, through his prophet Elisha, do for Naaman,
   and why? (See 2 Kings 5:1, 6 - 14.)

What response did it inspire from Naaman? (See 2 Kings
5:15 – 18.)

Discuss the ways in which Naaman's view of God changed
through this encounter. Do you think this was a lasting
change? Why or why not?

WHY MOUNT CARMEL?

Did you ever wonder why Elijah chose Mount Carmel as the place to confront
the prophets of Baal and Asherah? Consider the following facts about Mount
Carmel:

- It was more than a thousand feet high and already had an altar (in bad
  repair) dedicated to God (1 Kings 18:30).
- It symbolized fertile splendor (Isaiah 35:1 – 2), typically receiving more
  than thirty inches of rain per year. (*Carmel* means "God's vineyard.")
- It was the most heavily forested area in Israel, making it an ideal place in
  which to show the Canaanites (who worshiped fertility gods) who really
  was the one true God.
- It was probably desolate after more than three years of drought, so the
  people knew that God, or perhaps Baal, was angry. This formerly lush
  site was a good illustration that things were not well in Israel. (In other
  instances, Mount Carmel became withered as a result of curses — see
  Isaiah 33:9; Amos 1:2; and Nahum 1:4.)

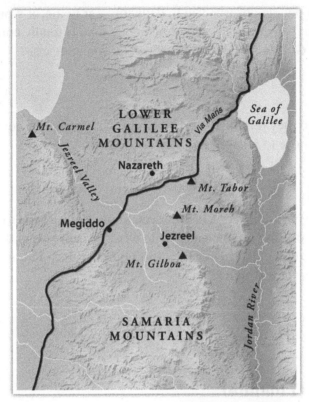

VALLEY OF JEZREEL

Faith Lesson (5 minutes)

God wants all the world to know that he is *Yahweh*, the one true God. He uses many different ways to bear witness of himself and open the eyes and hearts of those who do not know him. He also reveals himself through people who have put their faith and trust in him. Isaiah 43:12 says, "I have revealed and saved and proclaimed.... You are my witnesses ... that I am God."

Each of us will have opportunities to demonstrate that the God of the Bible is who he says he is. We reveal him as we obey his laws, as we reflect his ways in our thoughts and actions, and as we testify concerning what God has done — and is doing — in our lives. Conversely, when we are not totally committed to loving and obeying God, not only do we suffer, but what God desires to accomplish through our witness also suffers.

1. As people observe you in daily life — at home, at work, at play — what do they see? Someone who is totally committed to God and following his ways? Or someone else?

Are they reminded of who God is ... whether or not they choose to follow him? Why or why not?

2. If you, and every Christian you know, determined to be who God calls you to be and to do what he calls you to do, what might happen in our families? Our churches? Our communities? Our country?

Closing (1 minute)

Read the following Scripture passage aloud, then pray, asking God to give you the will to devote yourself to him wholeheartedly so that your everyday life will testify of God in such a way that others will recognize him as the one true God. Remember, the same God who demonstrated his power on Mount Carmel is very much alive today. He is willing to reveal himself in you and through you.

Memorize

> My mouth will tell of your righteousness,
>   of your salvation all day long,
>   though I know not its measure.
> I will come and proclaim your mighty acts, O Sovereign LORD;
>   I will proclaim your righteousness, yours alone.
>
> **Psalm 71:15 – 16**

The Battle for Our Hearts, Minds, and Souls

In-Depth Personal Study Sessions

Day One | Israel Loses Sight of Who God Is

The Very Words of God

> *You yourselves know how we lived in Egypt and how we passed through the countries on the way here. You saw among them their detestable images and idols of wood and stone, of silver and gold. Make sure there is no man or woman, clan or tribe among you today whose heart turns away from the LORD our God to go and worship the gods of those nations; make sure there is no root among you that produces such bitter poison.*

> **Deuteronomy 29:16 – 18**

Bible Discovery

A Royal Legacy of Idolatry

Since creation, people have had to choose whether they would worship and obey God or whether they would pursue other gods. After the Israelites crossed the Jordan River into the Promised Land, Joshua demanded that they make a definitive choice, and they insisted that they would worship and serve God to the exclusion of all others (Joshua 24:14 – 24). So how did all of Israel change from worshiping Yahweh to worshiping Baal? Why didn't their leaders stop them? As it turns out, their leaders were a large part of the problem. Consider the legacy of the kings of Israel.

1. In what evil did King Solomon participate late in his life, and how did God respond? (See 1 Kings 11:4 – 13.)

LEGACY OF A KING WHO HAD EVERYTHING

One could say that Solomon was the king who had it all. He was wealthy beyond imagination. He achieved world-renowned power and status. He ruled Israel during a period of relative peace and prosperity. God blessed him with wisdom beyond comprehension. And God granted him the privilege of building the temple of the Lord in Jerusalem.

When Solomon dedicated that temple, it was apparent that he loved the Lord and knew what it meant to follow him (1 Kings 8:22–53). When he blessed the people, he asked God to uphold Israel "so that all the peoples of the earth may know that the LORD is God and that there is no other" (8:60). He closed his blessing by reminding the people that their hearts must be fully committed to God and that they must live by all of his commands.

But Solomon was unfaithful to God in one crucial area: against God's command, he married foreign wives. Just as God had said they would, they turned his heart toward other gods (11:1–4). Because of his unfaithfulness toward God, Solomon's kingdom was given to one of his subordinates when he died (11:6–11). That subordinate was Jeroboam, who did nothing to restore a godly legacy to the kings of Israel.

2. Because of King Solomon's pursuit of other gods, God took ten tribes of Israel away from David's family line and made Jeroboam king of Israel. What did God promise Jeroboam if he would keep God's commandments? (See 1 Kings 11:37-39.)

3. What did Jeroboam, the first king of the northern kingdom of Israel, do to solidify his political position? (See 1 Kings 12:25-33.)

What impact did this have on God's people? (See 1 Kings
12:28 - 30; 15:34.)

How did God respond? (See 1 Kings 13:1 - 3, 33 - 34.)

4. Despite God's warnings, Jeroboam persisted in all the evil
    practices by which he had offended God. Read the following
    passages and notice how Jeroboam's legacy of evil persisted
    among future kings of Israel.

Scripture Text	Jeroboam's Legacy
1 Kings 16:25−26, 29−33	
2 Kings 10:31	
2 Kings 13:1−2	
2 Kings 13:10−11	
2 Kings 14:23−24	
2 Kings 15:8−9	

2 Kings 15:17–18	
2 Kings 15:23–24	

Reflection

In Deuteronomy 29, Moses warned Israel of the dangers of idolatry, saying, "Make sure there is no root among you that produces such bitter poison" (verse 18). For the kings and people of Israel, the worship of false gods became a bitter poison indeed. No matter how small and seemingly insignificant those first steps into idolatry were, they led to terrible consequences.

What confusion about God do you think leads Christians today away from a lifelong commitment of faithful obedience to him?

Why does the first step into sin so often play a significant role in someone's life?

What is a modern-day example of small "first steps" that have led (a) a Christian, (b) the church, (c) our nation or culture, and (d) you personally into greater sin? What has been the impact of such "first steps" on others, particularly subsequent generations?

Day Two | How Long Will You Waver?

The Very Words of God

> *"Has a nation ever changed its gods? (Yet they are not gods at all.) But my people have exchanged their Glory for worthless idols. Be appalled at this, O heavens, and shudder with great horror," declares the* LORD.
>
> **Jeremiah 2:11 – 12**

Bible Discovery

Confused by Two Masters

The legacy of idolatry planted by Solomon and nurtured by Jeroboam grew to maturity during King Ahab's reign. Ahab married Jezebel, a priestess of Baal from Phoenicia. She hated the God of Israel and tried to kill all of his prophets (1 Kings 18:4). Ahab, however, wasn't fully committed to God or to Baal. Like most of Israel, he worshiped both. He would honor God in one way, then turn to sacrifice to Baal and burn incense under Asherah poles. No wonder the people of Israel wavered in their commitment to God!

1. *Syncretism* is the combination of different forms of belief and practice. Israel practiced syncretism when they tried to combine God's truth with paganism. In God's eyes, this is as evil as outright unbelief. In the following Scripture texts, notice the indications that Ahab was serving both God and Baal.

    a. What did Ahab build, and how important did he consider God's laws to be? (See 1 Kings 16:30 – 33.)

    b. What were the names of Ahab's sons? Why would a committed worshiper of Baal have chosen these names? (See 1 Kings 22:40; 2 Kings 1:17; 3:1.) NOTE: The Israelites often used part of God's name in their children's names. So any biblical name ending with *iah* or *jah*, or beginning with *Jeho* or *Jo*, included a part of God's name.

2. Imagine what it must have been like for God to send Elijah, a prophet whose very name means "Yahweh is God," into this period of confusion about which deity to serve!

   a. What is the first thing Elijah said to Ahab? (See 1 Kings 17:1.)

   b. Given the fact that Baal was considered to be the god of rain, what message was God sending to Ahab via the man whose name meant "Yahweh is God"?

   c. What did Elijah do for the next three years? What message did God tell Elijah to give to King Ahab when he appeared again? (See 1 Kings 17:2 - 3, 7 - 9; 18:1.)

3. One would think that more than three years not just of drought, but of not even one drop of dew would have created a crisis of belief for Baal worshipers. Certainly they must have wondered if Baal was truly the powerful god who brought rain and fertility to the land, or if Jehovah was the true God.

   a. How did the people of Israel respond when Elijah asked them to choose which deity they would follow? (See 1 Kings 18:20–21.)

   b. When Elijah gave the people a way to see who was the true God, how did the people of Israel respond? (See 1 Kings 18:22–24.) NOTE: In addition to being the god who sent rain, Baal was also thought to be the god of fire and lightning.

   c. What do these responses say to you about the spiritual commitment of the people?

4. What finally answered the "Who is God?" question for the people of Israel? (See 1 Kings 18:36–40.)

THE TRUTH OF THE MATTER

During his reign, King Ahab and the Israelites tried to serve both Yahweh and Baal. Unwilling to commit to one or the other, they worshiped both. They would honor Yahweh, then go to high places to sacrifice to Baal, burn incense under Asherah poles, and participate in religious rites with prostitutes. Elijah knew that the values represented by Baal and God were contradictory. So he challenged the people of Israel to evaluate their actions — to consider the futility of trying to serve two masters — and to choose whom they would serve.

Jesus also addressed the importance of choosing whom to serve when he commented on the futility of serving both God and money: "No one can serve two masters," he said. "Either he will hate the one and love the other, or he will be devoted to the one and despise the other. You cannot serve both God and Money" (Matthew 6:24).

Reflection

It is amazing to realize how confused and uncommitted the people of Israel had become in their faith. God wants his people to know him: "Do men make their own gods? Yes, but they are not gods! Therefore I will teach them — this time I will teach them my power and might. Then they will know that my name is the LORD" (Jeremiah 16:20 – 21). The consequences that the sins of Israel's leaders had on God's people for generations ought to be a powerful warning to us to seek to know God and to obey him in every way.

> In which area(s) of your life are you inclined to serve a "god" other than the God of the Bible? (Consider materialism, pride, pursuit of pleasure or fame, etc.)

When a Christian tries to live in two worlds — the world of God and the world of Satan — what inevitably happens? Why?

What is the legacy of faith that you are leaving for other people? How might it differ from the legacy that you *want* to leave for others?

Memorize

Even while these people were worshiping the Lord, they were serving their idols. To this day their children and grandchildren continue to do as their fathers did.

2 Kings 17:41

Day Three | The Role of God's Prophets

The Very Words of God

Therefore, O house of Israel, I will judge you, each one according to his ways, declares the Sovereign Lord. Repent! Turn away from all your offenses; then sin will not be your downfall. Rid yourselves of all the offenses you have committed, and get a new heart and a new spirit.

Ezekiel 18:30 – 31

Bible Discovery

Speaking on Behalf of God

Through his servant Moses, God promised the people of Israel that he would send prophets to help them remain faithful to him in a

pagan world. These prophets would call God's people back to his
words and remind them of God's insistence on total allegiance.

1. Read Deuteronomy 18:14 - 22 and note what Moses reveals
    about God's prophets and why they were needed.

    a. What kinds of "prophets" would the Israelites find in
        Canaan, and how were God's people to respond to them?
        (See verse 14.)

    b. Why would God send prophets to speak to the people on
        his behalf, and where would these prophets come from?
        (See verses 15 - 16.)

    c. What words would the prophets speak, and what would
        happen to those who did not listen? (See verses 18 - 19.)

    d. What were the people of Israel to do to false prophets,
        and how were they to know which prophets truly spoke
        for God? (See verses 20 - 22.)

2. Elijah was the first of the prophets God sent to call his
    people back from their sinful ways.

a. How did Elijah know what to do and say, and how readily did he obey? (See 1 Kings 18:1 - 2, 7 - 15.)

b. How would the people of Israel have known that Elijah
was a prophet of God? (See 1 Kings 17:1 - 3, 7; 18:24,
36 - 39.)

Reflection

After God used Elijah in such a powerful way to reveal to Israel their
sinfulness in worshiping Baal, one might think that Elijah would
have had an easier life — a bit of a reward, perhaps, for his faithful
service. But Elijah was human, just as we are. He continued to face
the challenges of some very bad days and the exhilaration of good
days. He had to choose to walk with God as he dealt with his own
strengths and weaknesses. His experiences as God's prophet should
encourage us as we seek to be God's living witnesses.

Scripture Text	What Happened to Elijah	A Key Question for Us
1 Kings 18:45 - 46		When have you felt the strength of the Lord with you?
1 Kings 19:1 - 4		When have you felt this alone, powerless, and afraid?

continued on next page . . .

Scripture Text	What Happened to Elijah	A Key Question for Us
1 Kings 19:7–8		When has God strengthened you for a task he has set before you?
1 Kings 19:10		When have you been so honest with God?
1 Kings 19:11–13		When have you heard God so clearly?
1 Kings 19:14–18		When you are hurting, how has the knowledge of other faithful followers encouraged you?

As you seek to be a living witness for God, how can you cultivate a listening ear and a heart that is willing to obey whatever he commands?

If we don't listen to God's voice and obey him fully, what might be the consequences to ourselves? Our families? Our communities?

Day Four | High Places of Worship?
Or Shame?

The Very Words of God

> *They put God to the test and rebelled against the Most High; they did not keep his statutes. Like their fathers they were disloyal and faithless, as unreliable as a faulty bow. They angered him with their high places; they aroused his jealousy with their idols.*
>
> **Psalm 78:56 – 58**

Bible Discovery

Worshiping God in the High Places

The people of the ancient Near East customarily honored their gods by worshiping them on high places, and God allowed his people to build altars to him — and him alone — on high places as well. At times, God communicated with his people on high places. So God clearly allowed his people to employ cultural practices in their worship of him as long as those practices were used only in his service and had no pagan content. This study will help you gain a picture of the appropriate and inappropriate use of high places.

THE TEMPLE MOUNT AT JERUSALEM

1. In the following passages, note how the high places, even those that had been used for pagan worship, were used in service to God.

Scripture Text	High Place Events
Gen. 22:1–2, 9–14	
Ex. 19:20–22; 31:18	
Judg. 6:25–28	
1 Sam. 9:10–14	
1 Chron. 21:18–22:1	
2 Chron. 3:1	

2. When God's people went into the Promised Land, what had God told them to do with the Canaanites' high places of worship? (See Numbers 33:51 - 52; Deuteronomy 7:5 - 6.)

3. Often the Israelites didn't follow God's commands concerning the high places of pagan worship. What, in fact, did the Israelites do in the high places, and what were the consequences? (See 2 Kings 17:5 - 14.)

DATA FILE
The High Place and Altar at Dan

When Israel was divided into the northern kingdom (Israel) and the southern kingdom (Judah) in 920 BC, the high place at Dan was established as a worship site in northern Israel. Archaeological evidence indicates that it:

- Measured sixty-two feet square
- Was surrounded by a wall, with a staircase leading up to it
- Had buildings on it that housed the shrine or "idol" that was worshiped there

Three different high places were built on the same site.

Site 1

This site dates to King Jeroboam in the tenth century BC, who—after Israel split into two parts—wanted an alternative to the temple established by David and Solomon in Jerusalem. Jeroboam erected a golden calf on this site for the people to worship (1 Kings 12:26–30). This worship site had a platform sixty feet long and twenty feet wide and an altar in front of the steps. Avraham Biran, the archaeologist directing this excavation, discovered that the fire that destroyed the shrine of Jeroboam had also turned the stones red.

THE HIGH PLACE AND ALTAR AT DAN

continued on next page . . .

Site 2

Someone, probably King Ahab, rebuilt the high place and made it larger. The Israelites continued to sink deeper into pagan practices and values.

Site 3

During Jeroboam II's reign (ca. 760 BC), a large staircase and altar in front of this massive high place were added. Only parts of this altar, such as one of the horns that protruded from the four corners and part of the stairs leading to the altar, have been found.

During Jeroboam's reign, the prophet Amos predicted the final destruction of Israel because of its idolatry and pagan practices (Amos 3:12–15; 5:11–15; 8:14). Thirty years later, the brutal Assyrian army wiped the northern ten tribes from existence. Ashes and burn marks from a great fire on the altar and high place confirm Amos's prediction.

Reflection

God is a jealous God. Because he wants his people to show the world that he is the one true God, he cannot allow them to worship the gods of this world. Although he sometimes asks his people to reclaim certain aspects of culture for his purposes, he never wants them to bring shame and dishonor to his name by participating in the evil practices of culture.

What are some examples in our world of cultural traditions and practices that we can reclaim and use in God's service?

When we as Christians participate in our culture in order to influence and transform it, how vulnerable are we to adopting its values?

When you are engaged in your culture, in which specific area(s) do you struggle to be a godly influence without becoming an ungodly participant?

What steps do you take to ensure that you will live according to the values God has established?

Memorize

If in spite of this you still do not listen to me but continue to be hostile toward me, then in my anger I will be hostile toward you, and I myself will punish you for your sins seven times over.... I will destroy your high places, cut down your incense altars and pile your dead bodies on the lifeless forms of your idols, and I will abhor you.

Leviticus 26:27 – 28, 30

Day Five | What's in a Name?

The Very Words of God

A good name is more desirable than great riches; to be esteemed is better than silver or gold.

Proverbs 22:1

Bible Discovery

Understanding the Value of One's Name

During biblical times, a person's name was considered to be an expression of his or her identity. A good name meant more than a good reputation because it identified something about the life and character of its bearer. When a name was given to a person, it also implied knowledge of and authority over the person who was being named.

1. The following examples illustrate how, in the ancient world, a name identified something about the person's character or life circumstances.

   a. Why did Sarah and Abraham name their son *Isaac*, which means "he laughs"? (See Genesis 17:15 - 19.)

   b. Why was *Moses* given a name that sounded like the Hebrew for "to draw out"? (See Exodus 2:1 - 10.)

   c. Why did God give Jacob the name *Israel*, which means "he struggles with God"? (See Genesis 32:24 - 28; 35:9 - 10.)

2. What did God demonstrate when he changed Abram's name to Abraham and Jacob's name to Israel? (See Genesis 17:1 - 8; 35:9 - 10.)

   What did Pharaoh demonstrate when he renamed Joseph (Genesis 41:41 - 45)?

3. Elijah's name was particularly fitting for the message God sent him to convey to Israel during the spiritual turmoil of King Ahab's reign. The word *Elijah* is composed of two Hebrew words: *El*, which means "god" and is a general reference to deity, and *Jah*, which is one part of the word *Yahweh* and represents the most holy name of God. So Elijah's name meant, "Yahweh is (my) God." To say his name answered the question, "Who is God?"

   a. Why is Elijah's name so significant in light of the question he posed to the Israelites in 1 Kings 18:21?

   b. What do you think went through the minds of King Ahab, the priests of Baal and Asherah, and the people of Israel when Elijah stood before them and confronted them about their indecision?

   c. How does Elijah's prayer (1 Kings 18:36 – 37) relate to the meaning of his name?

4. When an angel came to Joseph and said that the virgin he was pledged to marry would give birth to a son, and that he was to name the baby "Jesus," which is a shortened version of "Yehoshua" or "Joshua," which means "Yahweh saves," what do you imagine he would have thought? How significant do you think it is that he named the baby Jesus? (See Matthew 1:20 – 25.)

Reflection

In light of the naming customs of the ancient Near East, God was
saying much more to Moses than "I know your name" when he said,
"I will do the very thing you have asked, because I am pleased with
you and I know you by name" (Exodus 33:17). He was saying, in
effect, "I know who you are, what you stand for, and how deeply
committed you are."

What is your identity before God?

If God were to give you a name that describes your walk with
him, what would it be? Is there another name that you would
prefer to have? Why?

Elijah, "Yahweh is (my) God," knew who God was. His very identity was a testimony to his commitment to God, and people saw
him live it out in a powerful way. What name would people who
see your daily walk with God give to you? Would it be a good
name that brings honor to God, or would it indicate something
else?

THE WAGES OF SIN

The ruins of Lachish stand as a monument to what can happen when a culture violates the standards revealed in God's Word and refuses to follow his ways. Lachish was once one of ancient Israel's largest cities. As you view the ruins of the city's massive gate, which is the largest gate structure found in Israel, you get a sense of the city's amazing strength and its importance as a key defensive point for protecting Jerusalem from invaders who might come up from Egypt. You can almost picture crowds of people walking along the cobblestone streets and conducting business in the compartments of the inner gate.

To understand what happened at Lachish, we must go back to about 920 BC, when Israel split into two parts: the northern ten tribes becoming the nation called Israel and the southern tribes becoming the kingdom of Judah. As we learn from 2 Kings 17, the people of Israel and Judah chose not to follow their God. They worried about prosperity and personal success instead of faithfulness and obedience to God. Caught up in the seductive religions of their culture, they repeatedly sought pagan answers, worshiped idols, and did other forbidden, "wicked things that provoked the LORD to anger" (verse 11).

In response, God sent prophets and seers to turn his people back to him. But after generations of warnings, the Israelites still refused to follow God and listen to his prophets. Finally, when his patience was exhausted, God allowed foreign nations to invade the land and punish his people.

In 722 BC, God allowed the cruel Assyrians (from the country we know as Iraq) to utterly destroy the ten northern tribes of Israel. Then the Assyrians turned their sights toward Judah. They captured all the fortified cities of Judah and marched on Lachish, the gateway to Jerusalem. During the siege and fall of Lachish, as many as fifty thousand people were brutally tortured and killed. The few prisoners who were taken to Assyria were led along by rings pierced through their lips. No one was spared, not even those who had followed God faithfully.

The king of Assyria, Sennacherib, marched his huge army to Jerusalem, where Hezekiah (king of Judah) reigned. But all was not lost. Hezekiah was unlike many of his predecessors. Instead of promoting idol worship, Hezekiah had removed high places, smashed sacred stones, cut down Asherah poles, and destroyed idols. He had obeyed God's laws and tried valiantly to impact his culture for God. So when Sennacherib mocked the faithfulness and power of the God of Israel, Hezekiah laid the whole situation out before God in the temple. He prayed that God would deliver his people "so that all kingdoms on earth may know that you alone, O LORD, are God" (2 Kings 19:19).

God heard that prayer. He had seen Hezekiah's commitment to him, and he promised to defend Jerusalem. That night, the angel of the Lord killed 185,000 Assyrian soldiers, and Sennacherib returned to Assyria without attacking Jerusalem.

We stand in a similar place today. Because of the immorality and evils of our culture, God's judgment hangs over us as well. He waits for those who are totally devoted to him to stand up and turn the hearts of the people back toward him.

Opening Thoughts (4 minutes)

The Very Words of God

> Hezekiah trusted in the LORD, the God of Israel. There was no one like him among all the kings of Judah, either before him or after him. He held fast to the LORD and did not cease to follow him; he kept the commands the LORD had given Moses. And the LORD was with him.

2 Kings 18:5–7

Think About It

We would have to admit that aspects of our culture are evil in God's sight. Although we know these things are an affront to God, we generally are content to coexist with them, and in some cases we even participate in them.

Why aren't we more active in opposing what God has declared to be evil? If we knew that within a short time God would send judgment on our culture unless people turned back to him — and that even the people who remained faithful to him would suffer — how might we live differently?

DVD Teaching Notes (23 minutes)

Lachish—a great city, a terrible fall

God's judgment at the hand of the Assyrians

Hezekiah's example

Our mandate to impact culture for God

DVD Discussion (7 minutes)

1. It can be difficult for us to comprehend the magnitude of
   the suffering the Assyrians inflicted on every living person
   in Lachish because of Judah's persistent sin. As you consider
   what happened there, what troubles or surprises you?

   If God deemed such a dreadful punishment necessary
   because of the sins of his people, how heinous must he have
   considered their sins?

2. What does the story of King Hezekiah reveal to you about
   the impact just one faithful, righteous person can have in
   the battle between good and evil?

EVIDENCE FILE
Tel Lachish: Its History Unfolds

Israel is dotted with a certain kind of hill called a *tel*. Each of these hills has steep sides, a relatively flat top, and looks a bit like a coffee table. The tels comprise multiple layers of settlements piled on top of each other. In the ancient world, later generations typically rebuilt their settlements on the same site as settlements that had been previously abandoned or destroyed. This customary process is referred to in Jeremiah 30:18, where we read how Jerusalem will be "rebuilt on her ruins," and in Jeremiah 49:2, which describes how Rabbah, an Ammonite city, will become "a mound of ruins." Some of the older tels in the more strategic locations of ancient Israel contain twenty or more layers of settlements!

TEL LACHISH

Tel Lachish—the main setting of this video—reveals the city's rich history. First settled more than four thousand years before Jesus' birth, it was destroyed and rebuilt at least six times. Between these total destructions, various changes in civilization occurred. For example, the layer of Hezekiah's time (700 BC) reveals massive fortification towers, a huge gate complex, and a palace. Another layer reveals the remains of the city's fiery destruction (587 BC). Tel Lachish and other tels are, in effect, a unique gift from God because they provide us with valuable insights that help us better understand his Word and interpret the Bible's message.

3. When people who follow God live in a culture that dishonors him, what other options do they have besides ignoring their responsibility to impact their culture for God?

What inevitably happens if they don't impact their culture?

Small Group Bible Discovery and Discussion (15 minutes)

God Expels a Rebellious and Hard-Hearted People

God has always commanded his people to worship him exclusively, to obey all of his commands, and to love him with all their heart, soul, and strength (Deuteronomy 6:3 - 5). But more often than not, God's chosen people disobeyed his commands and rejected him as their one and only God. Again and again they rebuffed his prophets, disregarded his warnings, and pursued the evil ways and worship practices of their neighbors. Finally, God's judgment fell on Judah and Jerusalem.

1. The events of the reign of Zedekiah, the last king of Judah, are recorded in 2 Chronicles 36:11 - 20.

   a. What kind of a king was Zedekiah at the beginning of his reign, and how did he change as time went on?

b. In what ways did the people, leaders, and priests also change during Zedekiah's reign?

c. In what ways did God respond to the sins of his people and why? How did his response change as time passed?

d. How complete was the destruction of Jerusalem and its inhabitants?

2. As is often the case with God, the end of the story isn't quite the end of the story. Notice how 2 Chronicles ends (36:21 – 23). Why would God do this, and what does it communicate to you?

3. Considering how much God loves his people and that his temple in Jerusalem was his chosen dwelling place on earth, what do you think it means that God was willing to destroy it because of the evil of sin?

What do you think this says about how seriously God views the sins of our culture — including any indulgence in sin by those of us who call ourselves Christians?

Faith Lesson (5 minutes)

Although many Christians today equate loving God with giving him
praise and worship, even a brief study of the prophets and kings
of Israel shows that to love God is to obey him. The bottom line is,
God hates sin. It is important for us to realize that total commitment
and obedience to God's commands were not just requirements for
God's people in ancient times. Jesus also said to his disciples, "If you
love me, you will obey what I command" (John 14:15).

Just as the people of Israel and Judah descended into unfaithfulness
by taking small steps of disobedience, Christians today are at risk of
becoming unfaithful to God when they take small steps into sin.

1. In which area(s) of your life do you find it hard to obey God
    completely? For example, which small steps away from God
    have you taken? (Be honest.)

2. In order to follow God faithfully, you must be willing to
    destroy any "high places" (sinful practices, habits, and
    "gods") to which you are devoted. Which "high place(s)" in
    your life needs to be confronted and destroyed?

3. What's keeping you from confessing and turning away from
    these sins?

Closing (1 minute)

King David knew what it was like to sin against God and to receive his forgiveness. In Psalm 32:5 he wrote, "I acknowledged my sin to you and did not cover up my iniquity. I said, 'I will confess my transgressions to the LORD' — and you forgave the guilt of my sin." Ask God to not only make you aware of sin in your life but to hate it as he hates it. Then confess your sin and turn back to him with a passionate commitment to obey him in all things. Invite him to use you and guide you in standing firmly against evil in your world.

Memorize

I acknowledged my sin to you and did not cover up my iniquity. I said, "I will confess my transgressions to the LORD" — and you forgave the guilt of my sin.

Psalm 32:5

The Battle for Our Hearts, Minds, and Souls

In-Depth Personal Study Sessions

Day One | Protecting What Is Most Important

The Very Words of God

> *Rehoboam lived in Jerusalem and built up towns for defense in Judah:*
> *Bethlehem, Etam, Tekoa, Beth Zur, Soco, Adullam, Gath, Mareshah, Ziph,*
> *Adoraim, Lachish, Azekah, Zorah, Aijalon and Hebron. These were fortified*
> *cities in Judah and Benjamin. He strengthened their defenses and put*
> *commanders in them with supplies of food, olive oil and wine. He put*
> *shields and spears in all the cities, and made them very strong. So Judah and*
> *Benjamin were his.*
>
> **2 Chronicles 11:5 – 12**

Bible Discovery

Guarding the Approaches to Jerusalem

The Israelites lived primarily in the mountains, clustered in towns
surrounding Mount Moriah and the city of Jerusalem. After David
established his kingdom, Jerusalem became the focal point of the
Israelites' religion and their national identity. So it was crucial to
protect the city from the enemies of Israel. Outposts such as Lachish
that guarded the approaches to Jerusalem had to be controlled.

1. Study the map of Israel on page 111, and notice the valleys
   and ridges that provided access routes through the mountains to Jerusalem. Also take note of the strategic cities that
   protected these routes to Jerusalem. Even before Jerusalem
   became the capital of Israel, the Israelites realized they
   needed to protect the territory surrounding it.

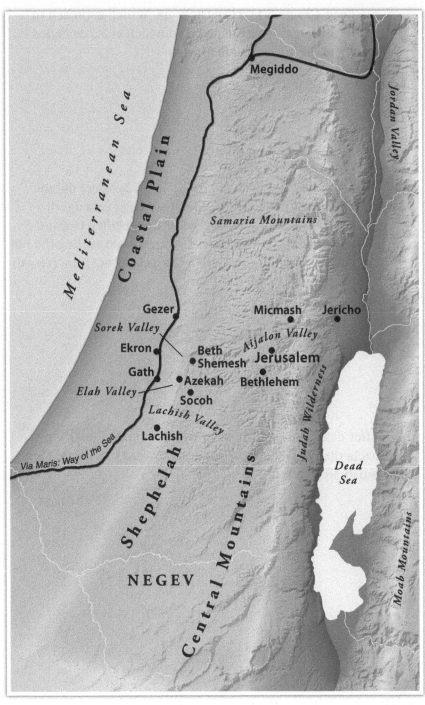

ISRAEL

a. Read 1 Samuel 13:23 - 14:1, 8 - 15. Which approach to Jerusalem was threatened, and which cities defended it? (Refer to the map to help you.)

b. According to 1 Samuel 17:1 - 3, 48 - 52, where did the Philistines pitch camp? Which strategic area did the Israelites need to protect? After David killed Goliath, how would you rate Israel's success in protecting the hill country near Mount Moriah (Jerusalem)? (Again, refer to the map for help.)

2. After defeating Lachish, from which direction did King Sennacherib of Assyria move his army toward Jerusalem? (See Isaiah 36:1 - 2.)

THE TRUTH OF THE MATTER
The Terrifying Assyrians

The Assyrian empire was located in Mesopotamia near the Euphrates River, in the region we know as Iraq. The Assyrians had such a bad reputation that Jonah fled when God commanded him to preach against them in their capital city of Nineveh (Jonah 1:1–3).

Known for their ruthlessness in battle and horrific treatment of captives, Assyrian soldiers were equipped with the latest weaponry—barbed arrows, catapults, and siege machines. The Assyrian army inflicted maximum suffering on its enemies in order to intimidate people who might otherwise resist. (Only individuals who had certain skills or abilities might be spared.)

Assyrian kings took great pride in recording their military conquests in writing (on tablets, clay cylinders, and obelisks) and in pictorial reliefs on stone slabs lining palace walls. Along with a recounting of victories won and plunder taken, archaeologists have found chilling lists of how the Assyrians tortured their captives. These included:

- Flaying (cutting skin into strips and pulling it off a living victim)
- Beheading
- Impaling (inserting a sharpened stake beneath the rib cage of a living victim, putting the stake into the ground so it stood erect, and leaving the victim hanging until the stake pierced a vital organ causing the victim to die)
- Burning people (especially babies and children) alive
- Severing hands, feet, noses, ears, tongues, and testicles
- Gouging out eyes

Reflection

Lachish was a strategic city because it was crucial to the defense of Jerusalem. If Lachish stood, Jerusalem would stand; if it fell, Jerusalem would fall. The relationship between Lachish and Jerusalem illustrates a spiritual truth that we need to be aware of as well: we must defend the less-central issues in order to protect the crucial beliefs and values of the Christian faith.

In what ways are Christians today — and the values of God — under attack from destructive influences? Why is it important for each of us, as believers, to recognize, fortify, and defend the "Lachishs" of our culture against the powerful forces of evil?

In the chart below, identify some "Lachishs" and "Jerusalems" of our day.

The "Lachishs"	The "Jerusalems"
The less-central issues that must be defended in order to protect the more crucial values	The key beliefs and values of the Christian faith

NOTE: "Lachishs" mentioned might include standing up for and defending purity and holiness in the face of pornography, integrity in the workplace as opposed to shady dealing, etc. "Jerusalems" might include: the sacredness of the family and the marriage union, the high standard of integrity to which God calls those who follow him, etc.

What will happen (and has happened) when we Christians let down our guard and surrender the "Lachishs" — the spiritual outposts — of our culture?

Which of these "Lachishs" are you committed to defend strongly?

Memorize

This is what the Lord *says:"Stand at the crossroads and look; ask for the ancient paths, ask where the good way is, and walk in it, and you will find rest for your souls."*

Jeremiah 6:16

CONFIRMING EVIDENCE
The Palace of a Great King

Assyria's kings were committed to more than military conquest. As part of their religious duty, they also constructed massive public buildings. Sennacherib, for example, built a new palace that he named the Palace without a Rival. According to his records, deportees from many conquered nations (probably including Israel) built it.

This palace, which was discovered during the late nineteenth century, contained more than seventy halls and chambers, all of them lined with stone panels (called *reliefs*) that depicted Sennacherib's accomplishments. Enormous statues of winged bulls guarded the doors of the hallway that led to the main chamber. Hallway walls were lined with panels commemorating the destruction of the cities of Judah, including the siege of Lachish. It is interesting to note that Sennacherib didn't reveal the whole story about his campaign against Jerusalem. The stone panels merely record that Sennacherib shut up King Hezekiah in Jerusalem like a bird in a cage!

Day Two | Hezekiah — Prepared to Defend God's People

The Very Words of God

> *This is what the LORD says:"Cursed is the one who trusts in man, who depends on flesh for his strength and whose heart turns away from the LORD.... But blessed is the man who trusts in the LORD, whose confidence is in him. He will be like a tree planted by the water that sends out its roots by the stream. It does not fear when heat comes; its leaves are always green."*

Jeremiah 17:5, 7 – 8

Bible Discovery

A Man of Action Who Trusted in God

King Hezekiah was a man of action — a faithful and gifted individual who had great foresight. He was a king who got the right things done. In preparation for Assyria's attack on Jerusalem, he combined wisdom, leadership, and extraordinary human effort to build a 1,748-foot tunnel that brought Jerusalem's water safely into the city from the spring of Gihon.

Although Hezekiah did everything possible to prepare his people to face the Assyrians, he also was humble before God and knew that victory was ultimately in God's hands, not his. When he faced the biggest crisis of his life, he acknowledged God's sovereignty and put himself under God's authority rather than counting on his own skills and abilities. He banked everything on the certainty that God would act on his people's behalf and show himself mighty in an otherwise hopeless situation.

1. According to 2 Chronicles 31:20 – 21, what kind of a leader had Hezekiah been for Israel, and how did God respond to him?

2. When Sennacherib, Assyria's king, began attacking the fortified cities of Judah, what did Hezekiah realize was happening and how did he respond? In what ways did he hinder
   the Assyrians, strengthen Jerusalem, and encourage God's
   people? (See 2 Chronicles 32:2–8.)

3. How did Sennacherib respond to Hezekiah and the Israelites'
   God? (See 2 Chronicles 32:9–19.)

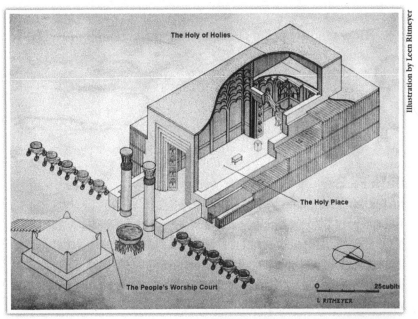

THE FIRST TEMPLE AT JERUSALEM

4. What actions did Hezekiah take in response to Sennacherib's challenges and mockery of Israel's God? (See Isaiah 37:1 - 2, 14 - 20.)

Are these the actions you would expect a king who had accomplished great things to take? Why or why not?

What does this reveal to you about Hezekiah's commitments and character?

5. How (and why) did God respond to Hezekiah's prayer? (See Isaiah 37:21 - 22a, 33 - 37.)

DATA FILE

Hezekiah's Amazing Water System

The spring of Gihon, which flowed out of a cave on the eastern side of the hill on which Jerusalem was built, provided the city's main water supply. (More than 24,250 cubic feet of water per day still flow from it.) As long as the cave's entrance was outside the city walls, the city's water supply was vulnerable to disruption by enemies.

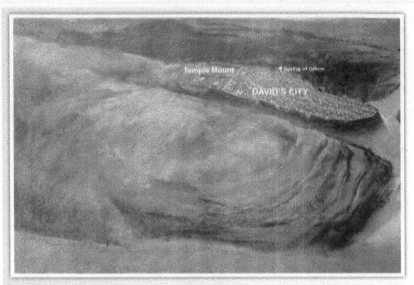

JERUSALEM OF DAVID AND SOLOMON

Before David captured the city about 1000 BC, the Jebusites living there dug a shaft from the city into the cave. Quite possibly Joab, David's commander, captured the city by entering the cave and climbing up the shaft. (See 2 Samuel 5:8 and 1 Chronicles 11:4–6.)

Although Hezekiah trusted God totally (Isaiah 37:14–20), he resolved to do everything possible to prepare his people to face the Assyrians. When he heard about the Assyrians' arrival in Judah, he ordered his workers to dig a tunnel from the cave through the ridge on which the city was built in order to bring water to the western side of the ridge—to the pool of Siloam within the city walls. Then he covered up the cave's opening (2 Kings 20:20; 2 Chronicles 32:2–4). Today, this extraordinary accomplishment—built more than seven hundred years before Jesus walked on the earth—still ranks as one of the engineering marvels of the ancient world. Here's why:

- Two teams of workmen, working from both directions, chiseled a tunnel barely two feet wide through solid rock, sometimes at points more than 150 feet underground, and met in the middle. And they did this without modern tools or instruments!

continued on next page . . .

- The tunnel is 1,748 feet long and has a drop of just twelve inches.
- Water more than waist deep still flows through the tunnel today.
- In 1880, boys playing in the tunnel discovered writing chiseled into the ceiling. Called the Siloam Inscription, it describes the dramatic moment when the two teams of workers met. Today, the inscription is in the Istanbul Archaeological Museum, having been removed from the tunnel when the Turks ruled Palestine during the late nineteenth century.

HEZEKIAH'S WATER TUNNEL

Reflection

Speaking for God, the prophet Jeremiah said that those who trust in themselves "will dwell in the parched places in the desert, in a salt land where no one lives" (Jeremiah 17:6). In contrast, those who trust in God "will be like a tree planted by the water that sends out its roots by the stream. It does not fear when heat comes; its leaves are always green" (17:8). Considering the crisis King Hezekiah faced, it is amazing that he did as much as he could and yet trusted God so completely. But the result speaks for itself: he faced a grave situation, and he did not fade in the heat of it. He remained strong in the Lord.

How do you respond to a crisis? To what extent does your trust lie in your abilities, gifts, resources, and/or "connections"? To what extent do you rely on God's help and guidance?

Does being faithful to God in the midst of crisis mean taking right action according to the Bible? Does it mean developing right attitudes? Does it mean giving God the opportunity to show himself powerful and giving him the glory? Think about how you do these things.

How do you find the proper balance between asking God for help and using the resources and talents he has given you to make the best decisions and take appropriate action?

Day Three | The Judgment of God Falls

The Very Words of God

To whom can I speak and give warning? Who will listen to me? Their ears are closed so they cannot hear. The word of the LORD is offensive to them; they find no pleasure in it. But I am full of the wrath of the LORD, and I cannot hold it in.

Jeremiah 6:10–11

ASSYRIA'S CONQUESTS

Circa 740 BC	King Tiglath-Pileser began plundering Israel (2 Kings 15:29). He destroyed many cities, brutally killed their inhabitants, and left Israel with only the capital of Samaria intact.
Circa 735 BC	King Shalmaneser marched on Samaria after Hoshea—the last king of Israel—refused to pay tribute to the Assyrians. The Assyrians slaughtered Samaria's inhabitants and destroyed the remainder of the northern kingdom.
722 BC	The ten northern tribes ceased to exist as a people. Israelites who remained in Israel were forcibly mixed with other religious and ethnic groups and became the hated Samaritans of the New Testament. Those who were deported disappeared from history.
Circa 700 BC	The new Assyrian king, Sennacherib, focused his attention on Judah, where he destroyed many cities. (He claimed to have destroyed forty-six walled cities and deported more than 200,000 captives.)

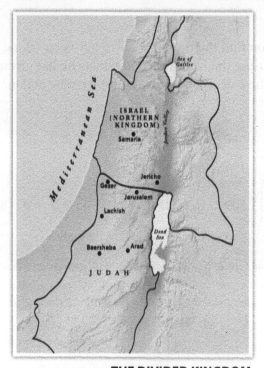

THE DIVIDED KINGDOM

Bible Discovery

When God's Wrath Cannot Be Contained

God is incredibly patient with his people, always ready to forgive. But he will not allow his people to persist in sin as if it is nothing. God's people belong to him, and when they are rebellious and refuse to heed his warnings, he will send judgment.

1. What was God concerned the Israelites would do once they settled in the Promised Land? What was the primary focus of his concern — what did he want them to remember? (See Deuteronomy 8:10 - 20.)

2. What did God promise would happen if the Israelites failed to obey him? (See Deuteronomy 28:45 - 52, 62 - 63.)

3. After Israel was divided, God sent his prophets to both Israel and Judah. Look up the following passages and summarize the message each prophet delivered. Note especially what God's people did that was so offensive to him.

Jer. 1:14 – 16; 2:1 – 9, 12 – 13	
The Prophet	
The Kingdom	
The Message	
Hos. 10:1 – 2, 5 – 10, 12 – 15	
The Prophet	
The Kingdom	
The Message	

4. Second Kings 17:14 – 23 describes the rebellious sins of Israel
    (and Judah) that finally led to God's judgment.

    a. Why do you think God considered it necessary to remove
        his people from the land he had provided for them?

    b. What warning does this convey to believers today?

WORTH OBSERVING
God Punishes People for Their Sins

The biblical reality that God hates sin and will eventually punish those who
persist in it is reinforced in the stories of the flood, Sodom and Gomorrah, the
conquest of Canaan, and the exile of the Israelites.

God's Judgment

God made the Sabbath principle central to his creation. As part of their rec-
ognition that God owned everything, the Israelites were to set apart the seventh day for the Lord. To violate the Sabbath day was a serious sin because it
denied God's sovereignty. Also, every seventh year the land was to lie fallow
and not be farmed (Leviticus 25:1 – 7). God promised to provide an abundant
crop in the sixth year so no one would be hungry during the following year.

Israel's illicit affairs with pagan gods started almost as soon as they arrived
in Canaan. When his people did not acknowledge him as their one true God,
he condemned their idolatry. As idol worshipers, his people violated the Sabbath day because they refused to recognize that they and their land belonged
to God. God warned them, in Leviticus 26:35, that if they continued to be
disobedient he would take their land from them so it would "have the rest it
did not have during the sabbaths you lived in it."

Continued disobedience finally caused God to bring judgment on his stiff-necked people, and he tore them out of the land he had given to them. In 722 BC, the Assyrians destroyed the people of Israel, the ten northern tribes (2 Kings 17:18–20). In 586 BC, the people of Judah were exiled to Babylon for seventy years — and the land received its Sabbath rest (2 Chronicles 36:15–21).

The Hope Promised

Although God allowed Assyria to take the people of Judah into exile, he did not forsake them, nor did he end his plan for their redemption. Second Chronicles 36 ends with optimism because the Israelites would return to their land and the temple would be rebuilt.

As it turned out, God's people experienced tremendous spiritual growth during the Babylonian captivity (586 BC). Without their temple, the Israelites learned that obedience is better than sacrifice (Psalm 40:6; Isaiah 1:10–20). They learned that if they did not obey all of God's commands, they would suffer the consequences. So they returned from Babylon with a renewed focus on God and the need to be faithful to him (Ezra 9:10–15).

Reflection

The great sin of God's people was that they "forgot" the Lord. They "forgot" that everything they enjoyed — fertile land and the blessings and success of life — was a gift from his almighty hand. They usurped God's sovereign authority and ignored his laws as if they had achieved their own success.

What are we acknowledging about God when we obey him, and what, then, are we saying about God when we choose not to obey him? How does this help you understand why God takes sin so seriously?

In what ways do our sins, and an unwillingness to confess them, affect our relationship with God and his willingness to bless us? In what ways do our sins affect our ability to impact our culture for God?

When God sends judgment on his people because of their sins, what is he encouraging them to do?

Memorize

Why has the land been ruined and laid waste like a desert that no one can cross? The LORD said, "It is because they have forsaken my law, which I set before them; they have not obeyed me or followed my law."

Jeremiah 9:12 – 13

Day Four | God Responds to Repentance

The Very Words of God

"Even now," declares the LORD, "return to me with all your heart, with fasting and weeping and mourning. Rend your heart and not your garments. Return to the LORD your God, for he is gracious and compassionate, slow to anger and abounding in love, and he relents from sending calamity."

Joel 2:12 – 13

Bible Discovery

Four Kings Who Prolonged God's Patience

In 722 BC, the ten northern tribes of Israel were destroyed when God expelled them from the land he had given to them. The southern kingdom of Judah, however, continued to exist for more than a century before falling to God's judgment at the hands of the Babylonians. Why did Judah last so much longer than Israel? Consider the work of several kings who — at least temporarily — brought the people of Judah back from the brink of disaster.

King Asa

1. What did King Asa do that pleased God and encouraged his people to seek the Lord? (See 2 Chronicles 14:2 - 7; 15:8 - 16.)

   What were the results of doing what was right and good in the eyes of God?

2. What prophecy did God send to King Asa through the prophet Azariah? (See 2 Chronicles 15:1 - 2.)

   How did King Asa regard this message of promise and warning early in his life (2 Chronicles 15:7 - 15) and later in his life (2 Chronicles 16:1 - 9)?

   How did God respond to Asa's change in approach?

King Joash

3. What did King Joash do to turn the people back toward
    God? (See 2 Chronicles 24:2 - 4, 8 - 14.)

    Who was Joash listening to during this time, and what
    impact did this counsel have on him?

4. What changed after the death of Jehoiada, the chief priest,
    and what was the result in Judah? (See 2 Chronicles
    24:17 - 25.)

    Who was Joash listening to during this time, and what was
    the impact of their counsel?

King Hezekiah

5. What did King Hezekiah do to restore the people's relation-
    ship with God? (See 2 Chronicles 29:1 - 10, 20 - 24, 35 - 36;
    30:1, 18 - 20.)

    How would you describe Hezekiah's spiritual insight and
    commitment to God?

6. What were the results of Hezekiah's commitment and work in Judah and Israel? (See 2 Chronicles 30:25 – 31:1.)

King Josiah

7. Instead of following false gods, what did King Josiah do? What was the result? (See 2 Chronicles 34:3 – 8, 14, 19 – 33.)

Reflection

These four kings of Judah, who were by no means perfect, took radical steps to guide their people back to God. Notice what they did personally in thought and action as well as what they did in their realm of authority to bring people back to God.

It's easy for us to think, *I'm not a powerful leader in government, so what can I do to impact my culture for God? What difference will my attitudes and actions make?* But each of us is here to help the world see who God is.

Which radical change(s) might you need to take — in your family, in your community, among your peers in the business world, etc. — to return to God so that those who see you can see who he is?

How deep is your commitment to pleasing God, to bringing him delight through your obedience and willingness to stand firmly for him and his truth in daily life?

How seriously should you take to heart God's promises to be
with the kings of his people as long as they "sought" him and
obeyed him?

What relevance do these promises have for your life — your
choices, your plans, your commitment to walk with God?

Memorize

*Return to the LORD your God, for he is gracious and compassionate, slow to
anger and abounding in love, and he relents from sending calamity.*

Joel 2:13

Day Five | God's Willingness to Forgive

The Very Words of God

*This is what the Sovereign LORD, the Holy One of Israel, says:"In repentance
and rest is your salvation, in quietness and trust is your strength, but you
would have none of it." ... Yet the LORD longs to be gracious to you; he rises to
show you compassion. For the LORD is a God of justice.*

Isaiah 30:15, 18

Bible Discovery

God Is Faithful to Forgive

Although our culture, not unlike the culture of ancient Israel, tends
to gloss over the reality of sin, God still takes sin seriously. So seriously in fact, that he sent his son Jesus Christ to redeem us from sin
by shedding his own blood on our behalf! When we are willing to
turn away from our sin and turn to God, just as the people of Israel
did under the rule of godly kings, God responds with mercy and
forgiveness.

1. God was so offended by his people's indulgence in sin that he was compelled to expel them from the Promised Land, yet he never stopped longing for repentance and never ceased to welcome a heart that turned toward him. As you read the following messages from God's prophets, what do you discover about the faithful, forgiving heart of God?

Scripture Text	The Heart of God toward His People
Isa. 30:15–18	
Isa. 55:7	
Jer. 5:1	
Jer. 33:4–9	
Ezek. 18:30–32	
Ezek. 36:22–36	
Hos. 14:1–7	
Mic. 7:18–20	

2. Generations after the dispersion of Israel and Judah, God sent his Son, Jesus Christ, to earth. Jesus died on the cross for the sins of humankind and rose again after three days in triumph over sin and death, thereby enabling all people to receive God's forgiveness. What do the following passages reveal about our sin and how we receive forgiveness and eternal salvation through Jesus Christ? (See Acts 5:29–31; Romans 6:20–23; 1 John 1:8–2:2.)

Reflection

Humankind's persistent pursuit of sin is a grievous sorrow for God, who longs to lavish his goodness on people who love, worship, and obey him with all their heart, soul, and strength. God himself says, "I revealed myself to those who did not ask for me; I was found by those who did not seek me. To a nation that did not call on my name, I said, 'Here am I, here am I.' All day long I have held out my hands to an obstinate people, who walk in ways not good, pursuing their own imaginations" (Isaiah 65:1 – 2). He still waits for those who will turn to him and pursue his righteousness.

What have you learned about God through this study?

In what ways has this study changed your view of your sins? Made you more willing to repent and confess your sins to God? Made you more willing to walk in obedience to him?

When it comes to dealing with our sins, why do we need God's help and forgiveness — a new heart and a new spirit?

What is God, through Jesus, willing to do for anyone who believes in Jesus and asks for forgiveness from his/her sins?

Memorize

If we confess our sins, he [God] is faithful and just and will forgive us our sins and purify us from all unrighteousness.

1 John 1:9

THE LORD IS MY SHEPHERD

Filmed in the Negev, the southern desert region of Israel, this video will help us better appreciate the meaning of Scripture passages that describe God as our *Shepherd*. It will also provide insight into the Israelites' wilderness experience, which is the source of much of the Bible's imagery and teaching. These images are important for us to understand because the Bible's inspired writers were part of a culture that is quite different from ours. They were Eastern (Hebrew) thinkers; we are Western (Greek) thinkers. Although it is difficult to describe these differences concisely, one key difference lies in our tendency to use abstract definitions (Western) and the Israelites' preference for concrete examples (Eastern).

For example, while we might define God as omnipotent and compassionate, the psalmist would say, "The LORD is my shepherd." The Bible comes alive when we begin to appreciate the meaning of the rich images in Scripture. We comprehend the Bible on a whole different level when we realize that the word pictures it contains, such as that of the Shepherd tending his sheep, are not just intellectual concepts but are true representations of God's nature and our relationship with him.

Because of their nomadic wanderings in the desert prior to entering Canaan, the Israelites thought of themselves as wilderness or desert people. Abraham, Isaac, Joseph, Moses, and even King David lived and worked in the desert for periods of time. In fact, the ancestors of the Hebrew people lived in tents, raised sheep and goats, and moved from place to place to feed their flocks in much the same way Bedouin people live today. Long after the Hebrews settled in the more hospitable land of Canaan, their wilderness experience continued to shape their identity and the images and metaphors they used to describe God and his relationship with them.

In this session, we will focus our attention on a series of faith lessons from the land and people of Israel's wilderness.

- We will discover that the shepherds who are leading a flock of sheep are children. Their father, the chief shepherd and head of their Bedouin group, keeps watch from a nearby hill as he handles other responsibilities of wilderness living. In a similar sense, Jesus — whom the Bible calls our "Chief Shepherd" — guides and watches over his "undershepherds," the leaders of his people.

- We will take note of several highlights from Psalm 23. Sheep, for example, listen to their shepherd's voice but run away from a stranger's voice, and sheep follow where their shepherd leads. Similarly, Jesus — our Good Shepherd — goes in front of us and asks us to follow him, just as he asked the disciples to follow him.

- We will see that a shepherd in the Negev can't take his sheep to green pastures of knee-high grass where they can feast for weeks. Instead, the shepherd must find enough pasture to satisfy the flock's need for food each day. Although the grass may not be abundant, the sheep don't worry about what they will eat next because their shepherd always guides them to new grass when they need it. Likewise, we need not worry about what will happen tomorrow because God is our Shepherd. We can trust him to provide all that we need each day.

- Finally, we will see scenes from a wadi, a usually dry canyon that can suddenly turn into a torrent of rushing water, so that we might understand why the psalmist would say, "God leads me to *quiet* waters" that will provide the refreshment we need.

Opening Thoughts (4 minutes)

The Very Words of God

> *The LORD is my shepherd, I shall not be in want. He makes me lie down in green pastures, he leads me beside quiet waters, he restores my soul. He guides me in paths of righteousness for his name's sake.*
>
> *Psalm 23:1 – 3*

Think About It

All of us have words that we commonly use to describe our knowledge of and experience with God. As Western thinkers, we tend to use abstract terms to describe God's attributes. Eastern thinkers, on the other hand, tend to use images and metaphors to describe God.

Which words would you use to describe the character of God? Now, consider the images or metaphors that also could describe God who possesses these characteristics. To help you do this, complete the sentence: God is like _____.

DVD Teaching Notes (16 minutes)

Discovering the wilderness

Shepherds and their sheep

Jesus—our Good Shepherd

DVD Discussion (7 minutes)

1. Place yourself in the wilderness setting of this video. Imagine being a Bedouin shepherd — no electricity, no running water, no telephone or television, no neighborhood supermarket with its assortment of fresh produce. How might such a lifestyle change your perception of and need for God?

THE JUDAH WILDERNESS

THE NORTHERN EDGE OF THE WILDERNESS

2. In what ways did the explanation of "green pastures" in the Negev help you understand the biblical image of God being our Good Shepherd who can be trusted to provide and care for his sheep?

3. Why is it so dangerous for sheep to drink from water located in wadis, and how does a shepherd protect his sheep from this danger?

How does this image parallel the risks people today face when they try to quench their spiritual thirst apart from the protection and guidance of the Good Shepherd?

WILDERNESS PASTURE

QUIET WATERS IN THE WILDERNESS

FOR GREATER UNDERSTANDING
Word Pictures of the Scriptures

The early writers and readers of the Bible used word pictures and symbolic actions rather than abstract definitions (such as "compassionate" and "omnipotent") to describe God and his relationship with his people. Note what the following word pictures reveal about the nature of God and our relationship with him.

Ps. 18:2	God is our "rock." He is steadfast, immovable, a sure place on which to stand and take refuge. God is our "fortress," a place of safety. God is our "deliverer" who saves us. He is our "shield" who protects us from harm. He is the "horn," a symbol of strength, of our salvation.
Ps. 100:3	God's people are portrayed as the "sheep" of God's pasture, meaning they will receive daily protection and sustenance from him.
Isa. 40:11	God is presented as a loving "shepherd." He takes care of his people like a loving shepherd cares for his or her flock. Even the weak and defenseless are secure in his tender care.
John 3:3	Jesus used the term "born again" to illustrate the spiritual change that occurs when a person accepts him as Lord and Savior. This word picture reflects the completely new person God creates through his salvation—a person who sees God's kingdom in a new light; a person who has a new hope, new goals, and a new understanding of spiritual truth.
John 6:35	Jesus, the "bread of life," offers spiritual food that will completely satisfy our hunger. He alone offers the spiritual truth that provides life.
John 8:12	Jesus is the "light of the world." He will provide spiritual light for anyone who follows him, so instead of stumbling in spiritual darkness his followers will be able to follow a clearly lit path.

Small Group Bible Discovery and Discussion (21 minutes)

The Lord Is My Shepherd

Psalm 23 is one of the most familiar passages in the Bible. Many of us have memorized some or all of it, yet we often overlook the profound message it expresses. So take a few moments to read these verses aloud together; then slowly and thoughtfully read it silently before answering the questions.

> *The LORD is my shepherd, I shall not be in want.*
>   *He makes me lie down in green pastures,*
> *he leads me beside quiet waters,*
>   *he restores my soul.*
> *He guides me in paths of righteousness*
>   *for his name's sake.*
> *Even though I walk*
>   *through the valley of the shadow of death,*
> *I will fear no evil,*
>   *for you are with me;*
> *your rod and your staff,*
>   *they comfort me.*
> *You prepare a table before me*
>   *in the presence of my enemies.*
> *You anoint my head with oil;*
>   *my cup overflows.*
> *Surely goodness and love will follow me*
>   *all the days of my life,*
> *and I will dwell in the house of the LORD*
>   *forever.*

1. Now that the scenes of the wilderness where the shepherds of Israel tended their flocks are fresh in your mind, which words or phrases in this psalm convey a new or deeper meaning to you? Explain what you have discovered.

2. What hope did the shepherd bring to the psalmist who faced the challenges of life?

   How clearly does the shepherd's care and provision as revealed through these images speak to our hope today?

   If you were to write a descriptive psalm to let people in your world know the hope you have in life because of how much God cares for you, which images from our world today might you use? (Go ahead, encourage each other to stretch your imagination a bit. In the word pictures of your world, God might be like a personal bodyguard, a wise coach, etc.)

3. In light of what "green pastures" in the Negev are like, how might you need to change your perception of the provision God gives *today* and what he promises to provide *tomorrow*?

   Why is this kind of faith in God often hard to live out in our world?

Which cultural pressures and lies must we confront in order
to truly trust God to meet our daily needs in this way?

In what ways do you think our view of a full, abundant life
(John 10:10) differs from how David, who had once been a
shepherd in the wilderness, viewed abundance?

4. Although he did not use a sheep/shepherd image, Jesus also
   spoke in word pictures when he taught about trusting in
   God's daily provision. (See Matthew 6:25 – 34.) In what ways
   do the images Jesus used here help you gain a better understanding of and greater confidence in God's faithfulness in
   providing for you?

Faith Lesson (6 minutes)

The image of God being our Shepherd is not easy for us to understand fully because few of us know anything about caring for sheep!
So let's continue to "unpack" this profound word picture so that we
can discover more of the Good Shepherd who loves us dearly and
invites us to be in close relationship with him.

1. In what ways does your Shepherd provide for you so that
   you do not want?

2. What are the green pastures and quiet waters of your life, the places where God nourishes your body and restores your soul?

3. Identify the paths of righteousness into which God leads you for his sake.

4. What is the valley of the shadow of death that strikes fear into your heart?

5. How does having a strong, faithful Shepherd to lead you through that valley help you face it?

6. In what ways does God comfort you, give you hope, and cause your cup to overflow?

7. What assurance do you have that you will dwell in the "house of the LORD forever"?

Closing (1 minute)

Read the following verses aloud. Then pray, thanking God for being your Shepherd. Ask him to help you trust him and follow him more closely. Ask him to help you keep your eyes on him and listen to his voice so that you can remain on the right paths and not become lost or discouraged.

Memorize

> *I am the good shepherd; I know my sheep and my sheep know me — just as the Father knows me and I know the Father — and I lay down my life for the sheep.*
>
> **John 10:14 – 15**

The Battle for Our Hearts, Minds, and Souls

In-Depth Personal Study Sessions

Day One | Getting to Know Our Shepherd

The Very Words of God

> *Trust in the LORD and do good; dwell in the land and enjoy safe pasture. Delight yourself in the LORD and he will give you the desires of your heart. Commit your way to the LORD; trust in him and he will do this: He will make your righteousness shine like the dawn, the justice of your cause like the noonday sun. Be still before the LORD and wait patiently for him.*

> **Psalm 37:3 – 7**

Bible Discovery

The Shepherd Reveals His Love for His Sheep

The image of God as the Shepherd of his people appears more than two hundred times in the Bible (more than fifteen times in the New Testament). Knowing that the Israelites, who had a long-standing cultural heritage as shepherds, would clearly understand the relationship of the shepherd and his sheep, God used it as a metaphor for his relationship with his people.

In ancient times, God's people readily understood how God loved and cared for them when he described himself as their Shepherd. For Christians today, it takes a little effort to understand God as our Shepherd. Read each of the passages on page 146, then write in your own words what the images of the shepherd and his sheep reveal to you about God and his people.

Scripture Text	How God Loves His Sheep
Ps. 78:51 – 55	
Ps. 95:6 – 7	
Isa. 40:10 – 11	
Luke 12:22 – 32	
Luke 15:3 – 7	
John 10:1 – 5	
John 10:14 – 15	

Reflection

If one characteristic of pagans is that they frantically chase after the necessities of life and worry about whether or not they will have enough for tomorrow (Matthew 6:31 - 34), then some of today's Christians are living as pagans! Yet Jesus calls those who follow him to go where their Shepherd leads and to trust him to provide for their needs.

In our culture, do you think it is possible to live "one day at a time," and trust God to lead and provide? Why or why not?

How is it possible to plan ahead and set goals while following the Shepherd?

Do you find it easy or difficult to believe that God cares deeply for you and that he will "shepherd" you well?

Now here's the test: if you had been an Israelite, how much manna would you have gathered? (See Exodus 16:13 – 20.)

As you think about the care a shepherd provides for his sheep, in which area(s) do you especially need God's care right now? How are you seeking his guidance so you can be on the right path? How are you asking him to provide for your needs? How carefully are you listening for his voice?

Memorize

Come, let us bow down in worship, let us kneel before the LORD our Maker; for he is our God and we are the people of his pasture, the flock under his care.

Psalm 95:6 – 7

THINK ABOUT IT
The Myth of Green Pastures

Although we might think that the "green pastures" David mentioned in Psalm 23 refer to tall, lush grasslands like those in North America and other locations, the truth is that such grasslands don't exist in Israel. The regions in Israel where shepherds live have two seasons: the rainy season from November through March (when even the desert becomes green) and the dry season from April through October when the landscape is brown. Even during the rainy season, the grasses remain short. Sheep that graze in the marginal areas of the wilderness receive enough nourishment for the moment ... but no more. Day to day, the sheep depend on their shepherd to lead them to the food and water they need.

In Exodus 16:4 – 5, 13 – 26, we read that God — the Good Shepherd — provided bread and quail from heaven so that his people had food to eat every day. The Israelites were to take what they needed for that day ... and no more. When some of the people took more than they needed — just to make sure they'd have enough for the next day — the food they tried to store became full of maggots and smelled awful. For forty years God, the Shepherd of Israel, provided manna to nourish his people.

Knowing that our human tendency is to worry about the future, Jesus also reminded his followers of how important it is to trust God to meet our daily needs. He taught that it is more important to seek God and his righteousness than to worry about our future needs. Because God is our Shepherd, he knows exactly what we need. We can trust him to meet our needs today ... and tomorrow. "Therefore," Jesus said, "do not worry about tomorrow" (Matthew 6:34).

Day Two | The Chief Shepherd: Committed to His Sheep

The Very Words of God

> *The LORD will guide you always; he will satisfy your needs in a sun-scorched land and will strengthen your frame. You will be like a well-watered garden, like a spring whose waters never fail.*

> **Isaiah 58:11**

Bible Discovery

Following in the Footsteps of the Shepherd

Perhaps the most remarkable characteristic of shepherds in the ancient Near East (and of shepherds in the region today) is the way they *lead* their sheep. They don't drive their sheep ahead of them as shepherds often do in other parts of the world. Instead, the sheep follow their shepherd to enjoy the places of nourishment, rest, and safety that the shepherd finds. The relationship of the shepherd to the sheep describes the relationship God desires to have with his people.

1. When the Israelites left Egypt and headed for the Promised Land, how was God like a shepherd to them? (See Exodus 13:20 - 22; 14:19 - 20.)

2. What does God desire to provide for his people? How is this like what a good shepherd would provide? (See Isaiah 49:9 - 10.)

3. What terms does God use to express his concern for the people of Israel who did not follow his ways? In what way does this imagery help convey his compassion, unfailing love, and concern for their well-being? (See Jeremiah 50:6, 17 - 19.)

4. When Jesus described himself as the Good Shepherd, what did he want to provide for his sheep, and what was he willing to sacrifice for his sheep that others will not sacrifice? (See John 10:10 - 15.)

5. When even one sheep loses its way, what is the shepherd willing to do for it? What does this reveal about God's love and commitment to his sheep? (See Matthew 18:12 - 14.)

DATA FILE
The Wadis of Israel

The wilderness of Israel is scarred by deep, riverbed canyons called *wadis* (Hebrew, *nahal*). Although the wilderness in Israel receives little rainfall, the central mountains receive a great deal of moisture during the winter months. The thin topsoil of the mountains cannot absorb all this water, which runs into the valleys to the west and runs through the wadis into the desert wilderness areas that lie to the east and south.

The runoff from the mountain rains is so great that the wadis quickly fill with raging torrents. The water roars through the wadis, cutting deep walls into them and sweeping away any animals or people in its path. These flash floods can occur when the sky is clear because the rains fall some distance away. Even today, these floods pose a great danger to shepherds and their sheep.

Wadis both hinder and help the shepherds. On the one hand, crossing the wadis is difficult and can be very dangerous. Sheep, which are undiscerning, will choose to walk in dangerous water. That's why the shepherd must *lead* the sheep. But, on the other hand, the flash floods that crash through the dry canyons leave behind quiet, refreshing pools that enable vegetation to grow and provide watering places for sheep. It is the shepherd's task to determine if these pools are safe for the flock to drink from and lie beside — if they are the "quiet waters" referred to in Psalm 23.

A WADI IN THE NEGEV   **FLOOD IN A WADI**

Reflection

Psalm 73:23 – 24, 27 – 28 doesn't specifically mention God as our Shepherd, but it gives us a beautiful picture of what it is like to walk in the care of the Good Shepherd. "Yet I am always with you; you hold me by my right hand. You guide me with your counsel.... Those who are far from you will perish.... But as for me, it is good to be near God. I have made the Sovereign LORD my refuge."

How do you picture God as your Shepherd? Does he go before you every day while you listen for his voice and follow where he leads? If not, how might your days be different if you focused your eyes on him and sought to follow his every leading with all of your heart, soul, and strength rather than seeking out your own "pastures"?

Take some time to review your walk with God — your experience in following the Good Shepherd, and ask yourself, *What kind of a sheep am I? And is this the kind of relationship I want with my Shepherd?* Write here what your next step might be to continue in or return to the direction you truly want to go.

Sometimes we think, *I've strayed too far from God, and I don't think I can get back to him.* In contrast to this assumption, what is true about the Good Shepherd's commitment to seek out and save every one of his "lost sheep"?

Day Three | Discovering God in the Wilderness

The Very Words of God

> *Remember how the LORD your God led you all the way in the desert these forty years, to humble you and to test you in order to know what was in your heart, whether or not you would keep his commands.... Know then in your heart that as a man disciplines his son, so the LORD your God disciplines you.*

Deuteronomy 8:2, 5

Bible Discovery

Tested and Transformed in the Wilderness

To journey through the wilderness is to face hardship, danger, uncertainty, hunger, and thirst. Even when closely following in the footsteps of the Shepherd, the way is not easy, but the sheep thrive under the Shepherd's faithful care. Before entering the Promised Land, the Israelites traversed the wilderness. The experience of following their Shepherd through the dangers of the wilderness transformed them, as it does us.

1. Some of Israel's greatest leaders also went through trying times in the wilderness. Under what circumstances did Israel's forefathers spend time in the desert wilderness before God called them to accomplish his mission for their lives? How did their wilderness experiences prepare them for God's purposes?

Leader/ Scripture Text	Wilderness Circumstances	Preparation for God's Purposes
Abraham/ Gen. 12:1–10; 13:1–4		
Moses/ Ex. 2:11–22; 3:1–12		
David/ 1 Sam. 23:13–24:2; 25:1–8; 2 Sam. 2:1–4		

THE NORTHERN EDGE OF THE WILDERNESS

2. Biblical writers understood that while God's people were in the desert, he took on the difficult task of nurturing and disciplining them so they would learn to follow and depend solely on him. Read Psalm 78:12 - 39, noting what God did to nurture his people's faith in him and how they responded.

3. Why did God want his people to remember their wilderness experiences as they prepared to enter the Promised Land? What had God tried to teach them about himself, as their Shepherd, during their journey through the wilderness? (See Deuteronomy 8:1 - 6, 10 - 18.)

4. When God spoke to his people through the prophet Jeremiah, what was it about their time in the wilderness that God longed to experience again? What led God's people to forget the lessons of the wilderness? (See Jeremiah 2:1 - 7.)

DATA FILE
The Wilderness of Israel

Much of Israel is rugged desert, which is referred to in the Bible as *wilderness*. The two most significant wilderness areas in Israel are the Judah Wilderness (or Judea Wilderness in New Testament times) and the Negev. These deserts contain more rock than sand, and some areas within them are mountainous. The wilderness deserts receive just enough rainfall during winter months to sustain nomadic shepherds and their flocks.

The Judah Wilderness

The Judah Mountains form the middle section of the central mountain range in Israel. On the eastern side of this mountain ridge, descending into the Great Rift Valley more than 1,300 feet below sea level, is the rocky wasteland of Judah. Little rain falls here, and the land is split by deep wadis formed by centuries of rain runoff. Because this wilderness borders fertile mountain ridges for more than fifty miles, villages such as Bethlehem were able to sustain both shepherds (like David) and farmers (like Boaz and Ruth). Shepherds lived on the desert's fringes; farmers worked the soil of the mountains.

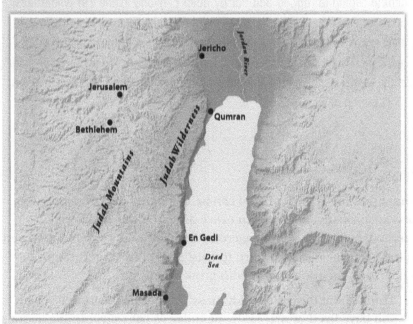

THE JUDAH WILDERNESS

continued on next page . . .

The Negev

The arid Negev (*Negev* means "dry") lies south of the Hebron Mountains that form the southern section of Israel's central mountain range. This desert receives fewer than eight inches of rainfall annually in the north and less than half that amount in the south. Except for a few settlements that use modern methods to catch rain runoff, only nomads live here.

Because the wilderness was so close to settled areas, many people seeking solitude or safety from authorities hid there. For example, in the Negev David hid from Saul (1 Samuel 26), John the Baptist isolated himself from religious practices of the day (Matthew 3), and Jesus faced the Devil (Matthew 4). People also associated the wilderness with the coming of the Messiah. Isaiah 40:3 reads, "In the desert prepare the way for the LORD; make straight in the wilderness a highway for our God."

The northern region of the Negev, from the Hebron Mountains to the Zin Wilderness, is good sheep country. Its rolling hills surround large, broad valleys such as the Valley of Beersheba in which Abraham settled. The Negev's central region is rugged and cut by deep canyons in the Zin Wilderness. Because the climate and terrain are so inhospitable — even to nomads — at least one scholar has suggested that the "valley of the shadow of death" mentioned in Psalm 23 may refer to the canyons here. The southern portion of the Negev is called the Wilderness of Paran in the Bible. This region is the most barren of all.

Reflection

Sometimes life is difficult and can be compared to the vast wilderness areas of ancient Israel. In every direction the landscape is parched, confusing, and dangerous. But God is our Shepherd — even in the wilderness. As we learn to trust and follow him through the wilderness, the roots of our faith grow stronger.

Think about difficult "wilderness" experiences through which you have lived or may be living today. What transforming lessons did you learn about yourself, your need for God, and his faithful provision and guidance during that time? To what extent are you living in light of those lessons today?

Once you have been transformed by the hardships of the wilderness, how do you stay transformed? What must you do to cultivate your ability to hear and follow your Shepherd's voice during wilderness experiences so the roots of your faith can grow stronger?

Memorize

Teach me, O LORD, to follow your decrees; then I will keep them to the end. Give me understanding, and I will keep your law and obey it with all my heart.

Psalm 119:33 – 34

Day Four | A Faithful Shepherd Keeps His Promise

The Very Words of God

Then the LORD said to Moses, "Write this on a scroll as something to be remembered and make sure that Joshua hears it, because I will completely blot out the memory of Amalek from under heaven."

Exodus 17:14

Bible Discovery
The Obedience of the Sheep Is Essential

Instead of obediently following the path of the Good Shepherd, we often pursue our own desires and choose our own paths. But God is patient and faithful. Even when we fail to do his bidding, God will fulfill his promises and accomplish his plan. Consider how God used the Israelites' experience with the Amalekites to teach his people the importance of obedience and to reaffirm his faithfulness in keeping his promises.

PROFILE OF A PEOPLE
The Israelites in the Wilderness

After God miraculously delivered the Israelites from Egyptian bondage, they wandered through the Negev and the Sinai Wilderness. When they reached the northern edge of the Negev, the Israelites sent spies into Canaan. After learning about giants and huge fortified cities, the people became afraid and refused to enter the Promised Land. Because of their disobedience and lack of faith, God commanded them to remain in the wilderness — "the vast and dreadful desert" (Deuteronomy 8:15) — for forty years, one year for each day the spies had been gone.

During these desert years, God taught his people faith and trust, preparing them to live obediently in the Promised Land *so that the world would know that he was God.* He also disciplined them for their lack of faith, disobedience, and complaining. Moses recorded that God humbled the Israelites so that they would learn to depend on him for everything, because "man does not live on bread alone but on every word that comes from the mouth of the LORD" (Deuteronomy 8:3).

Their forty years of wilderness wanderings significantly impacted the Israelites. Various Bible passages emphasize the lessons they learned:

- The psalmist reminded the Israelites of God's faithful love in the wilderness (Psalms 105:38–45; 107:4–9).
- The psalmist warned the Israelites against repeating their earlier sins (Psalms 81:11–16; 78:14–40).

- Jeremiah reminded the Israelites of what God had done for them and how they had disobeyed him and disregarded his warnings (Jeremiah 2:5 – 8; 7:21 – 26).
- Micah reminded them of God's previous blessings (Micah 6:3 – 5).
- The writer of Hebrews used the Israelites' wilderness wandering as an illustration of unbelief (Hebrews 3:7 – 19).
- Paul summarized some of the Israelites' sins in the wilderness and reminded readers to be careful (1 Corinthians 10:1 – 13).
- Jesus, when facing the tempter, used the lessons of the wilderness to defeat him. (See Matthew 4:4 and Deuteronomy 8:3; Matthew 4:7 and Deuteronomy 6:16.)

Today, the wilderness imagery of the Bible refers to our lives here on earth as we prepare for our "promised land" in heaven. It portrays difficult times in our lives when we learn to trust God. It offers a picture of God disciplining us for our sins and reminds us of the Messiah's eventual return. Truly the wilderness is still the place where we, God's people, learn that we cannot live on bread alone.

1. As the Israelites journeyed toward the Promised Land, what did the Amalekites do, and what was God's response? (See Exodus 17:8 - 16.)

2. Before they entered the Promised Land, what did God command the Israelites to do? (See Deuteronomy 25:17 - 19.)

   Who did God select for this important task, and how was it to be done? (See 1 Samuel 15:1 - 4.)

What did King Saul do to fulfill God's command? (See 1 Samuel 15:7 - 9.)

In what ways did King Saul's view of obedience differ from God's, and what was the result? What did King Saul fail to understand about obedience to God? (See 1 Samuel 15:13 - 26.)

3. About four hundred years after Saul failed to obey God's command regarding the Amalekites, how did Haman, a descendant of Agag, endanger the entire nation of Israel? (See Esther 3:1 - 6, 8 - 11.)

4. What opportunity did God, in his mercy, give to Esther, who was a descendant of Kish, Saul's father? (See 1 Samuel 9:1 - 2; Esther 2:5 - 11, 16 - 17; 4:12 - 17; 7:1 - 6, 9 - 10.)

Reflection

As Esther considered whether or not she would risk her life to save her people, her uncle Mordecai offered some advice that reflects a profound understanding of God's faithfulness in accomplishing his work among his people: "Do not think that because you are in the king's house you alone of all the Jews will escape. For if you remain silent at this time, relief and deliverance for the Jews will arise from another place, but you and your father's family will perish. And who knows but that you have come to royal position for such a time as this?" (Esther 4:12 - 14).

If Esther had known that her faithful obedience to God would fulfill a solemn promise he had made to his people centuries earlier, what do you think she might have thought about it? In what ways does the history of God's commitment to destroy the Amalekites change *your* understanding of his faithfulness?

How do Mordecai's prophetic words relate to what God may be calling you to do and be in your unique circumstances? Why has God placed you where you are today? For which person(s) or circumstance(s) might your faithfulness to obey God have an impact for his kingdom?

What does it mean to you that God can use your obedience to fulfill his faithfulness and to produce blessings for generations after you are gone?

Day Five | Leading with the Heart of God

The Very Words of God

I will give you shepherds after my own heart, who will lead you with knowledge and understanding.

Jeremiah 3:15

Bible Discovery

Undershepherds Answer to the Chief Shepherd

Some scholars believe that the practice of young shepherds (often girls) tending sheep under the watchful eyes of adults is the basis for the biblical picture of God — the Chief Shepherd — appointing undershepherds to care for his flock. The undershepherds are accountable to God for how they lead his flock.

1. God often spoke of King David as having a heart like his own. What early experiences in David's life may have nurtured such a heart? (See 1 Samuel 16:10 – 13.)

2. In what way was Moses exhibiting the heart of the Chief Shepherd when he helped the young shepherds who cared for their father's flock in Midian? (See Exodus 2:16 – 17.)

3. Ezekiel 34:1 – 16 is a powerful portrayal of God's heart as the Chief Shepherd of Israel. What does God want his undershepherds to do for his flock?

   Not all the leaders of God's people were good shepherds, however. For what did God condemn the undershepherds of Israel and why? (See Ezekiel 34:1 – 10.)

   What did God promise to do to the shepherds who had failed in their God-given responsibilities to care for the sheep he had entrusted to them? What did God promise to do for his sheep who had suffered under their care? (See Jeremiah 23:1 - 4; Ezekiel 34:11 - 16.)

What must those of us who are undershepherds (pastors, lay leaders, parents, teachers, older brothers and sisters, disciplers, sports coaches) learn from these passages about the importance of doing our work faithfully?

4. What was it about Peter that led Jesus to give him the responsibility to care for his sheep? (See John 21:15 - 17.)

What does this tell you about the expectations God has for those who are undershepherds, responsible to care for his flock?

5. What imagery did Paul use when speaking to the Ephesian elders about their responsibilities for the church, and what did he tell them to do? (See Acts 20:28 - 31.)

6. What guidelines did God, through Peter's writing, give to undershepherds who cared for his people? What did God promise would happen when Jesus — the "Chief Shepherd" — appears? (See 1 Peter 5:2 - 4.)

Reflection

Jeremiah 3:15 is a beautiful promise from God to his people: "I will give you shepherds after my own heart, who will lead you with knowledge and understanding."

How would you describe in your own words what it means to be an undershepherd after God's own heart?

What are the characteristics of an undershepherd who faithfully cares for God's flock? In which practical ways can you demonstrate these characteristics in daily life?

As an undershepherd, what should your attitude be toward those for whom you are responsible to lead with "knowledge and understanding"? And what ought to be the attitude of the sheep toward those who are responsible for leading?

Memorize

*Be shepherds of God's flock that is under your care, serving as overseers ...
eager to serve; not lording it over those entrusted to you, but being examples
to the flock. And when the Chief Shepherd appears, you will receive the crown
of glory that will never fade away.*

1 Peter 5:2 – 4

GOD WITH US

As far back as 3000 BC, a Canaanite city stood in the Negev where the small town of Arad sits today. In fact, the city existed when Abraham lived in the Negev. After the Canaanite city was destroyed, the Israelites rebuilt and fortified it for the defense of Israel's southern frontier. A unique series of historical events has preserved in Tel Arad a temple built to honor God.

When King Hezekiah came into power, he eliminated Baal worship and ordered the destruction of all shrines, altars, and high places. He wanted God's people to worship in Jerusalem, so even the high places dedicated to the worship of God were destroyed. Although the people in Arad apparently worshiped and honored Yahweh exclusively, they had to destroy their temple. Instead of tearing it down, however, they covered it with earth, which has preserved it for our viewing and helps us better understand how the Israelites worshipped God.

The temple in Arad was smaller in size than the temple in Jerusalem, but it had the same courts, furnishings, and altar. The temple in Arad is particularly valuable because the Babylonians completely destroyed Jerusalem in 586 BC, including Solomon's temple. The temple was important to God's people because it was the focus of their worship — the place where they offered sacrifices to God and where his presence lived.

God had made a covenant with Abraham to make him the father of a great nation and to give his descendants a land in which to live. In keeping with the customs of making a covenant, God asked Abraham to gather five animals — a heifer, goat, ram, pigeon, and dove — each of which Abraham cut into two parts from nose to tail and placed on the ground so that their blood flowed together in one stream. The custom called for both parties to walk in that blood, signifying that each would give his or her own life to keep the covenant. (To break a covenant was to invite one's own death as a penalty.) When God walked the "blood path," he showed his willingness to give his life to keep his covenant with Abraham. In effect, God said, "If this covenant is ever broken — by you or by me — my blood will cover the failure." After this time, animal sacrifices to God reminded God's people of his promise to forgive them and to cleanse them from their sins.

When two parties made a covenant, each received a stone tablet that summarized the covenant. In the case of God and Israel, the tablets contained the Ten Commandments. Each party then put their tablet into their most sacred shrine. Imagine how Moses felt when God gave him *both* tablets to put into the ark of the covenant! God was saying, in effect, "My sacred and holy place is exactly the same as your sacred and holy place. I love you so much that I'll come and live on the cover of the ark." Thus, God our Creator lived on the cover of a box that was placed in the Holy of Holies in the temple in Jerusalem.

When the Babylonians destroyed Jerusalem, God's presence left the temple and was later revealed through his Son, Jesus, who loved us enough to live on earth among us. After Jesus died as the sacrificial Lamb of the covenant, God's power and presence came to live within his believers. Just as God lived on the ark of the covenant, he now lives within each Christian. When people need to know that God is real and living among us, they no longer need to go to a temple made by human hands; they need only to look at us. What an opportunity! What a responsibility!

Opening Thoughts (4 minutes)

The Very Words of God

> Have them make a sanctuary for me, and I will dwell among them.... There, above the cover between the two cherubim that are over the ark of the Testimony, I will meet with you and give you all my commands for the Israelites.

> Exodus 25:8, 22

Think About It

As Christians, we often say that God is with us, that he makes his presence known to us. But how does God do this? Think through what you know of biblical history and identify some times when God's people have known that he was real and that he was with them.

How do we know that God is real today? What evidence of God's presence can we see?

DVD Teaching Notes (29 minutes)

Arad and its temple

God's covenant:

With Abraham

Moses and the Ten Commandments

Jesus, the covenant sacrifice

God's dwelling place today

COMPELLING EVIDENCE
Arad's God-Fearing People

Archaeologists believe that the inhabitants who lived in Arad nearly three thousand years ago worshiped only *Yahweh*. The excavation there has uncovered the following items:

- Potsherds with writing on them (*ostraca*) inscribed with the names of priests mentioned in the Bible and Yahwistic names (that contain part of God's name)
- Bowls inscribed "Sons of Bezalel" (Exodus 31:1–11)
- An offering bowl inscribed "Sacred for the Priests"
- A temple similar in design to Solomon's temple in Jerusalem

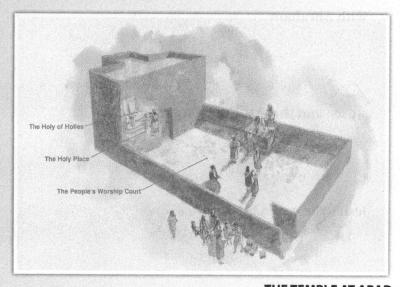

The Holy of Holies

The Holy Place

The People's Worship Court

THE TEMPLE AT ARAD

DVD Discussion (7 minutes)

1. As you observed the setting of Arad and its temple, what impressed you about the worship practices of God's people?

    Why do you think they built a temple to God at Arad?

2. We tend to think of the Ten Commandments as a list of "do's" and "don'ts" that God wants us to obey. How does learning that the Ten Commandments are a summary of God's covenant and a reminder of his love change how you think of them? And respond to them?

TEL ARAD

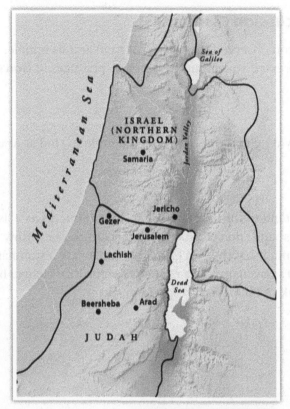

THE DIVIDED KINGDOM

3. It is an awesome realization to understand what the Israelites
   knew: that the ark of the covenant in the temple at Jerusalem was truly the dwelling place of God. In light of this fact,
   how do you respond to the realization that God now lives in
   Christians, that the Creator-God of the universe has chosen
   people to be his temple?

Small Group Bible Discovery and Discussion (10 minutes)

Jesus: The Covenant Sacrifice for Our Sins

God sealed his commitment to Abraham and his descendants by walking the blood path of the covenant, and that commitment was reinforced every time the Israelites sacrificed animals to God. Israel's sacrifices laid claim to the covenant God had made with Abraham to forgive their sins. However, even though God chose to live among his people on the ark of the covenant in the temple in Jerusalem, God's people broke their covenant with him again and again.

In response, God finally removed his presence from his people until he revealed it again through Jesus, his beloved Son. In Jesus, God reaffirmed his dedication to the covenant he had established with his servant Abraham. Jesus, the Lamb of God, gave his life — he sacrificed his blood when he died on the cross — to atone for the sins of everyone who had broken the covenant with God. Without exception, the writers of the New Testament believed that the Old Testament sacrifices of the covenant pointed to, and were fulfilled by, Jesus Christ.

1. Hundreds of years before Jesus came to earth to live among us, what did the prophet Isaiah say that the Messiah would do? (See Isaiah 53:4 - 6, 10.)

    In light of the covenant between God and Abraham, what greater understanding do you have for this passage and the meaning of the "guilt offering" the prophet mentioned in verse 10?

2. How do we know that people who lived during the time of Jesus knew of the need for sacrifice in order to restore the covenant with God and recognized that Jesus had come to be that sacrifice? (See John 1:29; 1 Corinthians 5:7; Hebrews 9:13 – 15.)

Faith Lesson (4 minutes)

Hebrews 9:15 refers to Jesus as "the mediator of a new covenant, that those who are called may receive the promised eternal inheritance — now that he has died as a ransom to set them free from the sins committed under the first covenant." By shedding his own blood, Jesus fulfilled the need for blood sacrifice to atone for sin that was required by the covenant between God and Abraham.

1. What does it mean to you that God was willing to shed his own blood in order to pay for your violation of his covenant?

The prophet Micah anticipated the end of the blood sacrifice and asked what sacrifices would be enough to please the Lord. He concluded that God has already revealed what he requires: "To act justly and to love mercy and to walk humbly with your God" (Micah 6:8). This paves the way for Romans 12:1, which urges believers to "offer your bodies as living sacrifices, holy and pleasing to God — this is your spiritual act of worship."

2. What does it mean to offer yourself as a "living sacrifice" to God? How eager are you to obediently walk with God?

DATA FILE

The Coming of Jesus—Fulfillment of a Promise

God's covenant with Abraham and his descendants demonstrated the *promise of God*. He declared his commitment to the Israelites by walking the blood path.

Through the tabernacle, ark of the covenant, and temple, God's people experienced the *presence of God*. God began restoring his presence among his people.

The tablets of the Ten Commandments sealed the *relationship between the people and their God*.

Although these commitments spectacularly demonstrated God's love, they anticipated an even greater act of love: the birth of God's own Son on earth. The person of Jesus would fulfill everything that had come before. God would walk with his people as he had walked with Adam and Eve. The blood of Jesus, the Lamb of God, would atone for the sins of those who believed in him. In Jesus, God would reaffirm his dedication to the covenant relationship he made with Abraham.

In Jesus, God fulfilled his promise to give his own life to seal the covenant he made with Abraham. For this reason, Jesus could say, "Do not think that I have come to abolish the Law or the Prophets; I have not come to abolish them but to fulfill them" (Matthew 5:17).

God's choice of the covenant to describe his relationship with his people highlights the extent of his deep love for us. Not only did the sovereign Creator of heaven and earth descend to be in relationship with sinful human beings, but he also offered his life to provide escape for the very people who would violate his covenant! People of the ancient Near Eastern cultures understood what a covenant was and recognized the indescribable gift of relationship God had given to those who believed in him. It should be no less for us.

Closing (1 minute)

Read the following verse aloud, then thank God for his faithfulness to his covenant with Abraham. Thank him for sending Jesus to be the sacrifice for the sins of all humanity. Ask God to help you recognize the terrible nature of sin and to truly offer yourself as a "living sacrifice."

Memorize

> *This is my blood of the covenant, which is poured out for many for the forgiveness of sins.*
>
> **Matthew 26:28**

THINK ABOUT IT
The Times of Daily Sacrifices

Although there is debate as to exactly which hours the early Israelites offered their sacrifices (see Numbers 28:3–8), we know that during Jesus' time the morning offering was made at the third hour, which is in midmorning (about 9:00), and the afternoon sacrifice was made at the ninth hour, which is in midafternoon (about 3:00). It appears that these times were established early in the history of the temple service. After Zerubbabel began rebuilding the Jerusalem temple (see Ezra 3:3; 9:5; Acts 3:1), daily prayers were said during these times as well. So for centuries God's people knew an offering was being made for their sins every day at midmorning (halfway between sunrise and noon) and midafternoon (halfway between noon and sunset).

Now consider the specific time of day when Jesus died on the cross. Matthew 27:46 says Jesus died at "about the ninth hour," which is at the time the afternoon sacrifice was being made at the temple. What significance do you think there is to the fact that these two events happened simultaneously? What was God saying?

The Battle for Our Hearts, Minds, and Souls

In-Depth Personal Study Sessions

Day One | God "Cuts" Covenants with His People

The Very Words of God

> *When Abram was ninety-nine years old, the LORD appeared to him and said, "I am God Almighty; walk before me and be blameless. I will confirm my covenant between me and you and will greatly increase your numbers."*
>
> **Genesis 17:1 – 2**

Bible Discovery

Covenants That Bind Relationships

In the ancient Near East, there was a special covenant form in which a greater party (often a king) established a relationship with a lesser party (often a vassal). The greater party determined the responsibilities of each, and the lesser party accepted or rejected the relationship. To establish a covenant meant more than making a legal agreement; it meant to be bound together in a permanent relationship. Thus, God used covenants to define and establish his relationship with his people.

The Bible passages on page 176 represent covenants God made with his people. For each, note (1) the person through whom God made the covenant; (2) why God, as the superior party, had the right to make the covenant; (3) what God promised within the relationship; and (4) any sign given as a symbol of the covenant.

The Covenant with ...	God's Right	God's Promise	The Sign
Gen. 9:8–17			
Gen. 15:4–21; 17:1–11			
Ex. 19:3–6; 24:3–8, 12; 31:18; 40:18–21			
2 Sam. 7:1–26			
Heb. 13:20–21; Luke 22:19–20; 1 Cor. 5:7			

DATA FILE
The Ark of the Covenant

The ark of the covenant was the most sacred object the Israelites had. Its main purpose was to hold the Ten Commandments, the tablets that summarized God's covenant with his people. It was also the place where the presence of God lived, so to come before the ark was to come into God's presence. Not only was the purpose of the ark unique among sacred objects in the ancient world, but the ark also had a unique origin and design.

God himself designed and specified the construction of the ark before any other sacred object (Exodus 25:10–22). The ark of the covenant:

- Was made of acacia wood commonly found in the Sinai Peninsula
- Was three feet nine inches long, two feet three inches wide, and two feet three inches high
- Had gold plating and a golden rim around the top
- Stood on four legs
- Contained two gold rings on each side so the Levites — the priestly tribe — could insert poles into it and carry it
- Had a cover (the mercy seat or atonement seat) made of pure gold
- Two cherubim — probably sphinxes with wings outstretched — were positioned on top of the lid. Their positioning may have expressed God's desire to cover his people in his sheltering arms.

The ark of the covenant assured the Israelites that the holy God of Abraham was sovereign over all things and was a protecting, forgiving presence in their lives (1 Chronicles 28:2; Psalm 99:1).

Reflection

Covenants were a readily understood and accepted practice in the ancient world. Everyone recognized the permanence and life-or-death consequences of keeping a covenant. Perhaps the "thick and dreadful darkness" that came over Abraham (Genesis 15:12) had to do with the realization that God had forever put his life on the line to establish his covenant with Abraham and that Abraham's life also was on the line to uphold that covenant. To take our relationship with God as seriously as a covenant requires will take some extra effort on our part because the ancient idea of a covenant isn't a familiar part of our culture and daily life.

Why do you think God made the effort to establish covenants with ancient people, and what does this reveal about him?

As you consider the "signs" God has given as symbols of his covenant promises, what do you notice?

How do these signs help remind you of God's faithfulness in upholding his covenants forever? Of your responsibilities in your relationship with God?

If you are a Christian, how does the significance of your participation in Communion change when you understand it to be a symbol of God's covenant with you?

How diligent are you in upholding the covenant you have made with God through the shed blood of Jesus?

What life changes do you need to make in order to honor your covenant relationship with God?

Memorize

> *But from everlasting to everlasting the L*ORD*'s love is with those who fear him, and his righteousness with their children's children — with those who keep his covenant and remember to obey his precepts.*

> **Psalm 103:17 – 18**

Day Two | God Gives the Ten Commandments

The Very Words of God

> *He [God] declared to you his covenant, the Ten Commandments, which he commanded you to follow and then wrote them on two stone tablets.*

> **Deuteronomy 4:13**

Bible Discovery

Called to a Life of Obedience

When God, through Moses, gave the ancient Israelites the Ten Commandments, he was doing much more than giving them a list of "do's" and "don'ts." God was establishing a covenant relationship with them that was based on his love for them. It's important for us to remember that the Ten Commandments don't stand alone; they are a summary of God's covenant relationship with Israel.

1. Before Moses received the Ten Commandments, what did God tell him to tell the people? (See Exodus 19:3 - 9.)

What was God offering to the people of Israel?

What was God's promise, and what were the people's responsibilities?

How did the people respond?

2. On the day God gave Moses the Ten Commandments, what did the people see, hear, and feel when they came out of the camp to meet with God? (See Exodus 19:16 - 20; 20:18 - 23.)

What was God's purpose in doing these things, and what impact did the scene have on the people?

What impact does this scene have on you and your commitment to obey God in all ways?

3. How did the people of Israel respond when Moses told them about the laws of the covenant? (See Exodus 24:1 - 8.)

4. After the people confirmed their commitment to God's covenant, God called Moses to the top of Mount Sinai, where
   he stayed with God for forty days and forty nights. At the
   end of that time, God gave to Moses the stone tablets of the
   covenant, written by God himself (Exodus 31:18). What had
   happened while Moses was with God? (See Exodus 32:1 – 8.)

How did Moses respond when he reached the Israelites'
camp? What do you learn about obedience to God from this
incident? (See Exodus 32:15 – 35.)

After all this, what did God agree to do again? What does
this reveal about him? (See Exodus 34:1 – 11.)

DID YOU KNOW?

Traditionally, Christians have believed there were two tablets of the Law:
one tablet (commandments 1 – 4) describing what our relationship with God
should be; the other (commandments 5 – 10) describing what our relationship with other members of the covenant should be. Although it is correct
to divide the commandments into these two categories, nothing in Scripture
supports the idea that each tablet had only a partial list of the Ten Commandments. Everything we know about the customs of making a covenant points
to all Ten Commandments being written on each tablet.

Reflection

It's all too easy for us to rationalize away our sins and not take obedience to God seriously. Yet our redemption through the blood of Jesus and our relationship with God is made possible by the covenants God established long ago. So set aside some time to read the Ten Commandments that God gave to Moses on Mount Sinai. Remember, this is God's expression of love for you.

And God spoke all these words:

*"I am the L*ORD *your God, who brought you out of Egypt, out of the land of slavery.*

"You shall have no other gods before me.

*"You shall not make for yourself an idol in the form of anything in heaven above or on the earth beneath or in the waters below. You shall not bow down to them or worship them; for I, the L*ORD *your God, am a jealous God, punishing the children for the sin of the fathers to the third and fourth generation of those who hate me, but showing love to a thousand generations of those who love me and keep my commandments.*

*"You shall not misuse the name of the L*ORD *your God, for the L*ORD *will not hold anyone guiltless who misuses his name.*

*"Remember the Sabbath day by keeping it holy. Six days you shall labor and do all your work, but the seventh day is a Sabbath to the L*ORD *your God. On it you shall not do any work, neither you, nor your son or daughter, nor your manservant or maidservant, nor your animals, nor the alien within your gates. For in six days the L*ORD *made the heavens and the earth, the sea, and all that is in them, but he rested on the seventh day. Therefore the L*ORD *blessed the Sabbath day and made it holy.*

*"Honor your father and your mother, so that you may live long in the land the L*ORD *your God is giving you.*

"You shall not murder.

"You shall not commit adultery.

"You shall not steal.

"You shall not give false testimony against your neighbor.

"You shall not covet your neighbor's house. You shall not covet your neighbor's wife, or his manservant or maidservant, his ox or donkey, or anything that belongs to your neighbor."

When the people saw the thunder and lightning and heard the trumpet and saw the mountain in smoke, they trembled with fear. They stayed at a distance and said to Moses, "Speak to us yourself and we will listen. But do not have God speak to us or we will die."

> *Moses said to the people, "Do not be afraid. God has come to test you,*
> *so that the fear of God will be with you to keep you from sinning."*
>
> **Exodus 20:1 – 20**

What new understanding of the severity of sin have you gained through this study?

How will you apply this knowledge to your everyday life?

What does God know about our inclination to sin, and what is he willing to do to keep us free from its bondage?

Even though Jesus came as the final interpreter of God's law, God still calls us to live obediently as his people. Jesus said, "If you love me, you will obey what I command" (John 14:15). Obedience is the way we demonstrate our relationship with God and our love for him (1 John 2:1 – 6).

How much do you love God? What are you willing to do to obey him and walk as he commands?

What changes do you need to make in your life in order to be more obedient (loving) toward God?

Memorize

If you love me, you will obey what I command.

John 14:15

Day Three Sacrifices in the Temple

The Very Words of God

> *Moses said to Aaron, "Come to the altar and sacrifice your sin offering and your burnt offering and make atonement for yourself and the people; sacrifice the offering that is for the people and make atonement for them, as the LORD has commanded."*

Leviticus 9:7

Bible Discovery

Atoning Sacrifices for Sin

The central act of worship for the Israelites was the shedding of blood. Primitive as that may seem, God established and continually strengthened his relationship with his people through the ritual of animal sacrifice. The animal sacrifices offered atonement for the people's sins and were an ever-present reminder of their covenant with God.

1. According to God's command, what daily sacrifices were the Israelites to make? (See Numbers 28:1 – 8.)

THE OUTER COURT OF THE TEMPLE AT ARAD

2. What did the animal sacrifices made by the priests on the altar of the Lord signify? (See Leviticus 17:5 - 7, 11; Hebrews 9:18 - 22.)

If you knew that atonement for your sins was being offered twice every day, and that each time a life was taken, how might your awareness of sin be different? How might it affect your desire to obey God's commands?

3. Describe the specifications God gave for the temple altar, which was to stand in the outer worship (or people's) court. (See Exodus 20:24 - 26; 27:1 - 8.) NOTE: The altar in Arad was built according to these specifications.

4. What was the purpose and location of the bronze Sea (basin)? (See Exodus 30:17 - 21.)

What kind of a reminder would this have been to the people, and to the priests, of God's holiness? NOTE: The bronze Sea of Solomon's temple is described in 2 Chronicles 4:2 - 5.

5. Which imagery found in Acts 22:14 - 16 and 1 Corinthians 6:11 is similar in function to the bronze Sea?

What kind of a reminder of God's holiness, then, should this practice be to us?

DATA FILE
The Temple Courts

The temple in Arad was built in a style probably influenced by Egyptian architecture and with materials similar to those used to build the average Israelite house. The temple in Jerusalem, on the other hand, was elaborately furnished and followed the Phoenician-Syrian temple design. Yet both temples contained the same courts and accomplished the same worship functions.

The Holy of Holies (God's Dwelling Place in Jerusalem)

This area contained the ark of the covenant, which held the tablets of the covenant (the Ten Commandments). In the temple in Arad, this area was reached by climbing two steps—symbolizing going up to God. Two standing stones were found in the temple in Arad. These stones may have represented the tablets of the Ten Commandments—God's covenant with Israel.

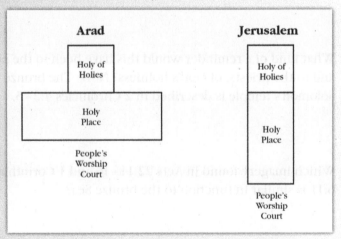

THE TEMPLES AT ARAD AND JERUSALEM

The Holy Place (Priests' Court)

Located between the worship court and the Holy of Holies, this rectangular room contained the table of showbread, golden lampstand, and the altar of incense. (The temple in Arad had two altars; the temple in Jerusalem had one.) The showbread was placed as an offering in the presence of God (Leviticus 24:5–9). This offering symbolized a thanksgiving gift to God as well as a request for his provision of food. The priests, on behalf of the people, ate the bread as a symbol of their relationship with God.

At Arad, the Holy Place was positioned so that its longest walls opened to the Worship Court on one side and the Holy of Holies on the other. (See the diagram of the two temples on page 186.) This style brought the people in the Worship Court closer to the priest and to God in the Holy of Holies. So the room was called the "broad room."

In the temple in Jerusalem, the shortest walls of the Holy Place bordered the Holy of Holies and the Worship Court, so the people were farther away from the priest and from God in the Holy of Holies. So the room was called the "long room."

The Worship Court (The People's Place)

This large outer court, in which the people stood to worship, contained the altar of sacrifice and the laver or basin (the bronze Sea).

PANORAMA OF THE TEMPLE AT ARAD

Reflection

The first time the priests ministered their sacrificial duties — sin offering, burnt offering, and fellowship offering — before the people of Israel, Moses and Aaron went into the Tent of Meeting. "When they came out, they blessed the people; and the glory of the LORD appeared to all the people. Fire came out from the presence of the LORD and consumed the burnt offering and the fat portions on the altar. And when all the people saw it, they shouted for joy and fell facedown" (Leviticus 9:23 - 24). In light of God's forgiveness of our sins and his desire to be with us, worship is always our appropriate response to God. Considering what the people of Israel had just witnessed, it is no wonder they fell down before God in worship.

What causes you to worship God? How important is worship in your daily life?

In the daily routines of the ancient Israelites, their sacrifices to the Lord and his ever-present forgiveness would certainly prompt worship. But what about us?

Which of your daily routines leads you to worship God?

What role might regular times of prayer, Bible reading, and fellowship with other believers play in reminding you of what God has done for you so that you will "be thankful, and so worship God acceptably with reverence and awe" (Hebrews 12:28)?

Memorize

> *Ascribe to the LORD, O mighty ones, ascribe to the LORD glory and strength.*
> *Ascribe to the LORD the glory due his name; worship the LORD in the splendor*
> *of his holiness.*
>
> *Psalm 29:1 – 2*

Day Four | The Holy Places of the Temple

The Very Words of God

> *Exalt the LORD our God and worship at his holy mountain, for the LORD our*
> *God is holy.*
>
> *Psalm 99:9*

Bible Discovery

God Reigns in Holiness

The altar and bronze Sea were positioned in the people's worship area of the temple, the part of the temple dedicated to cleansing from sin. The temple also had a Holy Place for the priests, where the table of showbread, golden lampstands, and altar(s) of incense represented aspects of God's relationship with his people. In the Holy of Holies was the ark of the covenant, God's place. The furnishings designed for these courts of the temple each had a specific purpose.

1. The offering of showbread represented a thanksgiving gift to God as well as a request for his provision. It was sometimes called the "bread of the Presence" because it was placed in the presence of God. Describe the table of showbread that God commanded Moses to make. (See Exodus 25:23 – 30.)

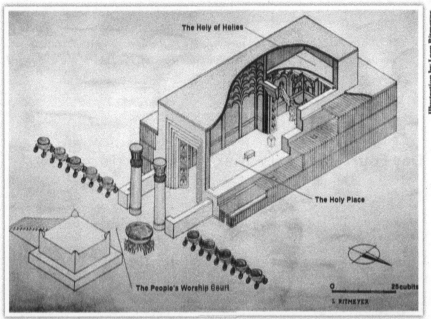

THE FIRST TEMPLE AT JERUSALEM

2. The golden lampstand stood in the Holy Place in front of the
    veil covering the Holy of Holies. It represented God's pres-
    ence in the tabernacle and later in the temple. What was
    unusual about the way the lampstand was to be made? (See
    Exodus 25:31 – 40; Numbers 8:3 – 4.)

    During which hours of the day were the priests to keep the
    oil lamps on the lampstand burning? (See Exodus 27:20 – 21.)

    How many of these lampstands did Solomon make for the
    first temple in Jerusalem? (See 2 Chronicles 4:7.)

3. The altar of incense was located in front of the entrance to the Holy of Holies. The temple in Jerusalem had one altar of incense; the temple in Arad had two. What does the offering of incense represent? (See Exodus 30:6 – 10; Psalm 141:2; Revelation 5:8.)

4. The ark of the covenant, which became the focus of God's presence among his people (Psalm 99:1), was kept in the Holy of Holies. Who was allowed into the Holy of Holies, and under what circumstances? (See Leviticus 16:2, 29 – 34.)

THE HOLY PLACE OF THE TEMPLE AT ARAD

DID YOU KNOW?

Rather than choosing a unique design for his temple in Jerusalem, God chose a well-known, older design that followed the Phoenician-Syrian temple design. Huram-Abi, the man Hiram, king of Tyre, sent to Solomon to supervise construction of the temple, was well skilled in this design style. In fact, Scripture reveals that he was "trained to work in gold and silver, bronze and iron, stone and wood, and with purple and blue and crimson yarn and fine linen" (2 Chronicles 2:14). He also was an expert engraver!

Reflection

Today many Christians know very little about the rituals God established or the functional equipment he designed for those who worshiped him in ancient times.

Why do you think God specified such tiny details concerning the temple? What did he want the worshipers to remember? To celebrate?

How might you benefit today from such remembrances and celebrations? For example:
As you pray, how does it help you to remember the offering of incense in the ancient temple and what it symbolized?

How might your appreciation for God's provision change if you kept in mind the image of the table of showbread placed before the presence of God?

In what way(s) are you to be like the golden lampstand shining out God's presence from the Holy Place?

Day Five | God's Presence in the World

The Very Words of God

> *Don't you know that you yourselves are God's temple and that God's Spirit lives in you?*
>
> **1 Corinthians 3:16**

Bible Discovery

God Reveals His Presence through Us

Christians today are to the world what the ark of the covenant and the temple were to Israel: God's dwelling place. God wants others to see in us convincing evidence of who he is. He wants his presence to be so visible in us that the world may know that he is God.

1. How near to his creation was God when he first created the world? What changed? (See Genesis 3:8, 23 – 24.)

2. Despite the rampant evil of humanity's sin, how do we know God watched and remained concerned for the people of the earth? (See Genesis 6:5 – 8; 7:1; 11:1 – 5.)

    How does this help you understand God's desire to establish a covenant of redemption with people?

3. What was the main purpose of the temple in Jerusalem? (See 2 Chronicles 5:7, 11 – 6:2; 7:1 – 3.)

What happened to God's presence because of Israel's unbelief? (See Ezekiel 10:18 - 19.)

How did God restore his presence among his people? (See John 1:1, 14.)

In what way does God choose to reveal his presence today? (See 1 Corinthians 3:16 - 17.)

PROVOCATIVE EVIDENCE
Where God Dwells

The Scriptures reveal some remarkable parallels between God's home in heaven and his former home on earth in the temple in Jerusalem:

Heaven	Temple
God's dwelling place (2 Chron. 6:21)	God's dwelling place (2 Chron. 6:1 – 2)
God surrounded by cherubim (Rev. 4:6 – 8; Ezek. 1:6, 10)	God surrounded by figures of cherubim (2 Chron. 3:10 – 13)
God surrounded by his heavenly hosts (Rev. 5:11)	God surrounded by his earthly hosts (Num. 2)
God is seated on a throne (Rev. 4:2 – 5)	The ark is God's throne (Ps. 99:1)
Altar representing the blood of the saints (Rev. 6:9)	Blood is sprinkled on the altar (Lev. 1:10 – 11)
Prayers of the saints viewed as incense (Rev. 5:8)	Priest met with God at the altar of incense (Ex. 30:1, 6)
Sea of crystal (Rev. 4:6)	Sea of bronze (1 Kings 7:23)

Reflection

In our culture today, Christians are God's dwelling place. We are the way God reveals his presence to the world. Our mission, like that of the ancient Israelites, is to be a light to the world so that the people who see us will see God. How, then, should we live so that the world may know that he is God?

What do people see when they see you? Does the light of God's presence shine brightly in your life?

Do you love in such a way that people know you belong to God? (See John 13:34 – 35.)

What will people remember about you and what was important to you? Are you leaving behind a God-fearing legacy like the people of Arad did?

What will you begin doing today to more effectively present the reality of God's presence to the world around you? Be specific!

Memorize

You are the light of the world. A city on a hill cannot be hidden. Neither do people light a lamp and put it under a bowl. Instead they put it on its stand, and it gives light to everyone in the house. In the same way, let your light shine before men, that they may see your good deeds and praise your Father in heaven.

Matthew 5:14 – 16

DATA FILE
Covenant Forms

Ancient Near Eastern covenants, especially those between unequal parties, formed complex relationships. Many factors had to be considered: the right of the greater party to make the covenant, obligations of each party, penalties and benefits of the relationship, and the relationship's history. So, covenantal documents were usually quite long. God's covenant with Israel through Moses, for example, is recorded in the Torah—the first five books of the Bible. God's covenant with believers in Jesus is described in all sixty-six books of the Bible.

Covenants were carefully recorded and preserved. They were to be read regularly and always obeyed. Moses, for example, wrote down the words of God's covenant with his people in the Torah and commanded that it be read every seven years (Deuteronomy 31:9–13, 24–26). The summary document—the Ten Commandments—was stored in the most sacred place: the ark of the covenant, God's earthly throne.

In order to make sense of covenants, people followed a certain pattern that governed the materials contained in a covenant, including its content and form. A summary document representing the entirety of the relationship and following the accepted form of a covenant document was also provided.

Keeping in mind that God cut covenants as the superior party so that he alone determined their content, let's briefly review the components of the covenant God made with the Israelites.

The Preamble
It identified the two parties of the covenant. In the Torah, God established the identities of the parties in the creation story. He was the Creator, and Israel was his creation. In the covenant summary (the Ten Commandments), he said simply, "I am the LORD your God" (Exodus 20:2).

The Historical Prologue
The history leading to the cutting of the covenant was recited to prove the right of the superior party to make it. In the Ten Commandments, for example, the summary is simply, " … who brought you out of Egypt, out of the land of slavery" (Exodus 20:2).

Requirements (Commandments)

The Torah contains 613 of the requirements God placed on the people with whom he was in relationship. He placed even more obligations on himself. In summarizing the commandments, these requirements were simplified to ten (Exodus 20:3–17). Some scholars have noted that Jesus reduced his summary to just two obligations (Matthew 22:37–40).

Blessings and Curses

Keeping a covenant brought specific rewards and breaking it brought specific penalties. The Torah, for example, contains many blessings and curses.

The Summary Document

The short summary document, which could be easily read and stored, summarized the entire covenant and so represented the total relationship between the parties. Normally in Near Eastern culture, two summary documents were made; each party kept one in a sacred place. So it seems clear that each tablet of the Ten Commandments contained all of the commandments. One copy was God's; the other belonged to the people of Israel. Part of the purpose of the ark of the covenant was to hold the Ten Commandments, the summary of God's covenant with his people.

BIBLIOGRAPHY

History

Connolly, Peter. *Living in the Time of Jesus of Nazareth.* Tel Aviv: Steimatzky, 1983.

Ward, Kaari. *Jesus and His Times.* New York: Reader's Digest, 1987.

Whiston, William, trans. *The Works of Josephus: Complete and Unabridged.* Peabody, Mass.: Hendrickson Publishers, 1987.

Wood, Leon. Revised by David O'Brien. *A Survey of Israel's History.* Grand Rapids, Mich.: Zondervan, 1986.

Jewish Roots of Christianity

Stern, David H. *Jewish New Testament Commentary.* Clarksville, Md.: Jewish New Testament Publications, 1992.

Wilson, Marvin R. *Our Father Abraham: Jewish Roots of the Christian Faith.* Grand Rapids, Mich.: Eerdmans, 1986.

Young, Brad H. *Jesus the Jewish Theologian.* Peabody, Mass.: Hendrickson Publishers, 1995.

Geography

Beitzel, Barry J. *The Moody Atlas of Bible Lands.* Chicago: Moody Press, 1993.

Gardner, Joseph L. *Reader's Digest Atlas of the Bible.* New York: Reader's Digest, 1993.

General Background

Alexander, David, and Pat Alexander, eds. *Eerdman's Handbook to the Bible.* Grand Rapids, Mich.: Eerdmans, 1983.

Butler, Trent C., ed. *Holman Bible Dictionary.* Nashville: Holman Bible Publishers, 1991.

Edersheim, Alfred. *The Life and Times of Jesus the Messiah.* Peabody, Mass.: Hendrickson Publishers, 1994.

Archaeological Background

Charlesworth, James H. *Jesus within Judaism: New Light from Exciting Archaeological Discoveries.* New York: Doubleday, 1988.

Finegan, Jack. *The Archaeology of the New Testament: The Life of Jesus and the Beginning of the Early Church.* Princeton, N.J.: Princeton University Press, 1978.

Mazar, Amihai. *Archaeology of the Land of the Bible: 10,000 - 586 BCE.* New York: Doubleday, 1990.

To learn more about the specific backgrounds of this DVD series, consult the following resources:

Avigad, Nahman. "Jerusalem in Flames — The Burnt House Captures a Moment in Time." *Biblical Archaeology Review* (November - December 1983).

Barkey, Gabriel. "The Garden Tomb — Was Jesus Buried Here?" *Biblical Archaelogy Review* (March - April 1986).

Ben Dov, Meir. "Herod's Mighty Temple Mount." *Biblical Archaelogy Review* (November - December 1986).

Bivin, David. "The Miraculous Catch." *Jerusalem Perspective* (March - April 1992).

Burrell, Barbara, Kathryn Gleason, and Ehud Netzer. "Uncovering Herod's Seaside Palace." *Biblical Archaeology Review* (May - June 1993).

Edersheim, Alfred. *The Temple.* London: James Clarke & Co., 1959.

Edwards, William D., Wesley J. Gabel, and Floyd E. Hosmer. "On the Physical Death of Jesus Christ." *Journal of American Medical Association (JAMA)* (March 21, 1986).

Flusser, David. "To Bury Caiaphas, Not to Praise Him." *Jerusalem Perspective* (July - October 1991).

Greenhut, Zvi. "Burial Cave of the Caiaphas Family." *Biblical Archaeology Review* (September - October 1992).

Hareuveni, Nogah. *Nature in Our Biblical Heritage.* Kiryat Ono, Israel: Neot Kedumim, Ltd., 1980.

Hepper, F. Nigel. *Baker Encyclopedia of Bible Plants: Flowers and Trees, Fruits and Vegetables, Ecology.* Ed. by J. Gordon Melton. Grand Rapids, Mich.: Baker, 1993.

"The 'High Priest' of the Jewish Quarter." *Biblical Archaeology Review* (May - June 1992).

Hirschfeld, Yizhar, and Giora Solar. "Sumptuous Roman Baths Uncovered Near Sea of Galilee." *Biblical Archaelogy Review* (November - December 1984).

Hohlfelder, Robert L. "Caesarea Martima: Herod the Great's City on the Sea." *National Geographic* (February 1987).

Holum, Kenneth G. *King Herod's Dream: Caesarea on the Sea.* New York: W. W. Norton, 1988.

Mazar, Benjamin. "Excavations Near Temple Mount Reveal Splendors of Herodian Jersualem." *Biblical Archaeology Review* (July – August 1980).

Nun, Mendel. *Ancient Stone Anchors and Net Sinkers from the Sea of Galilee.* Israel: Kibbutz Ein Gev, 1993. (Also available from *Jerusalem Perspective.*)

_____. "Fish, Storms, and a Boat." *Jerusalem Perspective* (March – April 1990).

_____. "The Kingdom of Heaven Is Like a Seine." *Jerusalem Perspective* (November – December 1989).

_____. "Net upon the Waters: Fish and Fishermen in Jesus' Time." *Biblical Archaeology Review* (November – December 1993).

_____. *The Sea of Galilee and Its Fishermen in the New Testament.* Israel: Kibbutz Ein Gev, 1993. (Also available from *Jerusalem Perspective.*)

Pileggi, David. "A Life on the Kinneret." *Jerusalem Perspective* (November – December 1989).

Pixner, Bargil. *With Jesus Through Galilee According to the Fifth Gospel.* Rosh Pina, Israel: Corazin Publishing, 1992.

Pope, Marvin H. "Hosanna: What It Really Means." *Bible Review* (April 1988).

Riech, Ronny. "Ossuary Inscriptions from the Caiaphas Tomb." *Jerusalem Perspective* (July – October 1991).

_____. "Six Stone Water Jars." *Jerusalem Perspective* (July – September 1995).

Ritmeyer, Kathleen. "A Pilgrim's Journey." *Biblical Archaeology Review* (November – December 1989).

Ritmeyer, Kathleen, and Leen Ritmeyer. "Reconstructing Herod's Temple Mount in Jerusalem." *Biblical Archaeology Review* (November – December 1989).

_____. "Reconstructing the Triple Gate." *Biblical Archaeology Review* (November – December 1989).

More Great Resources
from Focus on the Family®

Volume 1: Promised Land

This volume focuses on the Old Testament—particularly on the nation of ancient Israel, God's purpose for His people, and why He placed them in the Promised Land.

Volume 2: Prophets and Kings of Israel

This volume looks into the nation of Israel during Old Testament times to understand how the people struggled with the call of God to be a seperate and holy nation.

Volume 3: Life and Ministry of the Messiah

This volume explores the life and teaching ministry of Jesus. Discover new insights about the Son of God.

Volume 4: Death and Resurrection of the Messiah

Witness the passion of the Messiah as He resolutely sets His face toward Jerusalem to suffer and die for His bride. Discover the thrill the disciples felt when they learned of His resurrection and were later filled with the Holy Spirit.

Volume 5: Early Church

Capture the fire of the early church in this fifth set of That the World May Know® film series. See how the first Christians lived out their faith with a passion that literally changed the world.

Volume 6: In the Dust of the Rabbi

"Follow the rabbi, drink in his words, and be covered with the dust of his feet," says the ancient Jewish proverb. Come discover how to follow Jesus as you walk with teacher and historian Ray Vander Laan through the breathtaking terrains of Israel and Turkey and explore what it really means to be a disciple.

Volume 7: Walk as Jesus Walked

Journey to Israel where the 12 disciples walked the walk their rabbi Jesus taught them. Examining the culture and the politics of the first century, Ray Vander Laan opens up the Gospels as never before.

FOR MORE INFORMATION

Online:
Go to ThatTheWorldMayKnow.com

Phone:
Call toll-free: 800-A-FAMILY (232-6459)
In Canada, call toll-free: 800-661-9800

More Great Resources
from Focus on the Family®

Volume 8: God Heard Their Cry

Just when it seemed that Pharaoh could not be defeated, God provided for His People in ways they never could have imagined. Join historian Ray Vander Laan in ancient Egypt for his study of God's faithfulness to the Israelites—and promise that remains true today.

Volume 9: Fire on the Mountain

When the Israelites left Egypt, they were finally free. Free from persecution, free from oppression, and free to worship their own God. But with that freedom comes a new challenge—learning how to live together the way God intends. In this ninth set of That the World May Know® film series, discover how God teaches the Israelites what it means to be part of a community that loves Him, and the lessons we can begin to live out in our lives today.

Volume 10: With All Your Heart

Do you remember where your blessings come from? In Exodus, God warned Israel to remember Him when they left the dry desert and reached the fertile fields of the promised land. But in this tenth volume of That the World May Know® film series, discover how quickly the Israelites forgot God and began to rely on themselves.

Volume 11: The Path to the Cross

Discover how the Israelites' passionate faith prepares the way for Jesus and His ultimate act of obedience and sacrifice at the cross. Then, be challenged in your own life to live as they did by every word that comes from the mouth of God.

Volume 12: Walking With God in the Desert

Are you going through a difficult period of life? The loss of a loved one? Unemployment? A crisis of faith? During these desert times, it's easy to think God has disappeared. Instead, discover that it's only when we are totally dependent on Him that we find Him closer than ever and can experience God's amazing grace and provision.